How to Use the Timex Sinclair Computer

Jerry Willis and Deborrah Willis

dilithium Press
Beaverton, Oregon

10   9   8   7   6   5   4   3   2   1

Library of Congress Cataloging in Publication Data

Willis, Jerry.

How to use the Timex Sinclair computer.
Includes index.
1. Timex 1000 (computer) – Programming. 2. Sinclair ZX81 (Computer) – Programming. 3. Basic (Computer program language) I. Smithy-Willis, Deborrah. II. Title.

QA76.8.T48W54 1983   001.64   83-5128
ISBN 0-88056-113-0 (pbk.)

SuperCalc™ is a registered trademark of the Sorcim Corp.
VisiCalc™ is a registered trademark of VisiCorp.
Etch-a-Sketch is a trademark of Ohio Art.
Apple II is a registered trademark of Apple Computer, Inc.
ATARI 800 is a registered trademark of Atari, Inc.
PET is a registered trademark and VIC is a trademark of Commodore Business Machines, Inc.
Rubik's Cube is a trademark of CBS Toys.

Cover Design: Anton C. Kimball

Printed in the United States of America

dilithium Press
8285 S.W. Nimbus, Suite 151
Beaverton, Oregon 97005

7049968

Table of Contents

Chapter 1 Well, What Do We Have Here? 1

Chapter 2 Setup and Installation 15

Chapter 3 How to Get Your Computer Up and Running 23

Chapter 4 Loading Programs into theComputer 37

Chapter 5 Saving Programs on Cassette 47

Chapter 6 Programming in BASIC 51

Chapter 7 More BASIC 73

Chapter 8 Peeking and Poking Around 99

Chapter 9 Selecting Accessories for Your Computer 107

Chapter 10 Sources of Additional Information 117

Appendix A Error Report Codes 121

Index 123

An Important Note

The publisher and the authors have made every effort to ensure that the computer programs and programming information in this publication are accurate and complete. However, this publication is prepared for general readership, and neither the publisher nor the authors have any knowledge about or ability to control any third party's use of the programs and programming information. There is no warranty or representation by either the publisher or the authors that the programs or programming information in this book will enable the reader or user to achieve any particular result.

CHAPTER 1

Well,
What Do We Have Here?

This book was written for the novice computer user who has yielded to temptation (or responded to all those ads) and purchased one of the little computers designed by Sinclair Research Limited of England.

Sinclair Research designed a basic but functional computer that will do amazing things considering its modest price. From 1980 until 1982 the computer was sold as the Sinclair ZX81. The computer was heavily marketed throughout Europe where it sold very well. It sold even better in the U.S. where full page color ads in many popular magazines urged you to send in your $99 and look for the ZX81 in the return mail.

The ZX81 is now manufactured in Scotland in a plant owned and operated by Timex, the watch manufacturer. In September of 1982 Timex began selling its own version of the computer through thousands of retail outlets. The Timex version is called the Timex Sinclair 1000. The ZX81 and the 1000 are essentially the same computer. The only major difference is in "memory" capacity. The 1000 has a larger memory which means it can "remember" more and can use larger programs than the ZX81. All the examples in this book will run on either computer.

The book is also applicable to an earlier Sinclair computer, the ZX80 and an unauthorized copy of it, the Microace. However, our primary focus is on the ZX81 and the Timex Sinclair 1000 computers. The abbreviation TS1000 will be used to refer to the computer in this book. This book was written for the beginning computer user with little background in computer science or electronics who has access to a Sinclair or Timex computer. It should be a helpful, convenient means of learning about the computer. We wrote the book with the following objectives in mind:

1. To introduce you to the computer and its basic components, what they do, and how they work together. (Chapters 1, 8, and 9)

2. To provide an overview of the things you can do with your computer. (Chapter 1)

3. To give step-by-step instructions on how to set up or "install" your computer and tell you how to get it "up and running." (Chapters 2 and 3)

4. To describe how to load and save programs on standard audio cassettes. (Chapters 4 and 5)

5. To introduce the novice to the BASIC computer language. (Chapters 6 and 7)

6. To provide information on how to select, buy, install, and use popular accessories for the computer. (Chapter 9)

7. To provide information on other sources of information about your computer such as magazines, books, and user's groups. (Chapter 10)

Figure 1.1 The Timex Sinclair and accessories. *Courtesy of Timex Computer Corporation.*

If you are eager to get started using the computer move ahead to Chapter 2. The remainder of Chapter 1 will deal with the potential uses of the computer and how it works.

WHAT CAN YOU DO WITH IT?

Many people are downright skeptical about the computer. It is inexpensive; even when compared to other home computers it is tiny, and it is used mainly by first time computer owners. It may be inexpensive and tiny, but it is a real computer that works. In fact, it uses the same Z80 computer "chip" or integrated circuit that is found in many business computers costing thousands of dollars. With nearly half a million units sold throughout the world it is obvious that people are finding them useful.

COMPUTER LITERACY

In spite of its low price the computer works in essentially the same way as the bigger, more expensive computer systems. It can cost from $150 to $500 to attend a good course or workshop

Figure 1.2 The Z80 integrated circuit that is the heart of the TS1000. *Photo courtesy of Zilog Corporation.*

on computer literacy where you learn the fundamentals of computer usage. Carl Landen, an insurance agent in the Southwest bought his TS1000 because he felt the need to learn something about computers. He spent $99 on the computer and used a spare black and white television as his video display. He spent another $59 on a new tape recorder when an old one that had been banging around the house for years proved unreliable. Carl also spent around $45 on books about his computer, and he spent $78 on several different programs. For his investment he got what he wanted. He learned how to run a computer, how to write short programs, and how a computer operates. Eight months after buying the TS1000 he spent over $2000 on one of the small business oriented computers. He uses it regularly in his business. The skills he learned on the TS1000 formed a solid foundation for his current work with a bigger, more expensive computer.

The TS1000 can be your hands-on computer literacy course. Our guess is that over 40% of the people who buy the computer do so in order to learn about how computers work. It is a fine computer for that. Much of what you learn as you use the TS1000 will transfer to other larger, more versatile computers.

BASIC PROGRAMMING

In order to program the TS1000 you need to know its language. The TS1000 uses BASIC as its programming language. BASIC stands for Beginners All-Purpose Symbolic Instruction Code. There are many different computer languages in use today, but BASIC is by far the most popular. BASIC is actually a family of languages. There are many different versions. The BASIC used by the TS1000 is very powerful, and it has several features that make it easier to learn than some other popular versions. If you want to learn how to program a computer in BASIC the TS1000 is currently the least expensive computer with a full size or relatively complete BASIC. If you master the TS1000 version of BASIC it will not be difficult to learn how to write programs in other dialects (or versions) of BASIC as well. The only major drawback to the TS1000 as a computer for learning BASIC is the keyboard. It is tiny and requires considerable digital dexterity to use. If you are a confirmed touch typist be prepared for a shock when you try to use the keyboard. Hunt and peck typists, on the other hand, are less inhibited by the keyboard.

MACHINE LANGUAGE PROGRAMMING

It is also possible to write programs for the TS1000 in a computer language called Z80 machine language. This is a versatile language and one that is used primarily by commercial programmers. It is very difficult to learn, and the TS1000 is not well suited to work in machine language. A computer with the features and programs needed to learn machine language programming costs at least $270 today. If the higher price is enough to make you willing to tolerate some inconvenience, there are learning aids and books that will help you use the TS1000. *Mastering Machine Code on Your ZX81* by Toni Baker is a book on programming in Z80 machine language written specifically for the TS1000. It is published in England by Interface Publications and in the U.S. by Reston Publishing Company. A newer book, *Machine Language Made Simple for ZX80 and ZX81*, is available from Gladstone Electronics, 901 Fuhrmann Boulevard, Buffalo, New York 14203. Gladstone also sells a program called an *assembler* that is very useful if you plan to do much work in machine language. The ZXAS Machine Code Assembler is $9.95 and comes on a cassette. Remember, however, that learning to write machine language programs is hard. Start with BASIC and put off tackling machine language until you have some experience under your belt. It is estimated that less than 5% of TS1000 owners use their computer for machine language programming.

FUN AND GAMES

If you set aside 8 hours a day to play all the games that are available for the TS1000 computer, it would probably take a year to play each game just once. And by the time you finished playing all the ones that are available now hundreds of new ones would be available. Our guess is that 35% of TS1000 owners use the computer primarily for fun and games. Several magazines publish at least one or two game programs for the TS1000 in each issue (see Chapter 10), and hundreds of small (and not so small) companies sell game programs for the TS1000. The commercial programs generally come on a cassette. You buy the cassette and use a tape recorder to load the game's instructions into the memory of the computer. Once the instructions are loaded into the computer's memory the computer can be told to "Run" the program. Here is a descriptive sample of some of the games that are available for the TS1000:

SUPERINVASION. This $15 game is very similar to the invader games so popular in video arcades. Bad guys from outer space come marching down to earth and you must shoot them down with your laser weapon or be overrun and destroyed. Created by Softsync, Inc. (P.O. Box 480, Murray Hill Station, New York, New York 10156).

ZXCHESS. This $25 program will play a mean game of chess. You can select any of seven levels of play, and if you get stuck the computer will even recommend a move for you. It is also available from Softsync.

ZETATREK. You are the pilot of a small fighter spacecraft that patrols the polar region of an area near your space station base. Diabolical Lizardmen attack you on every turn and you must fly your craft skillfully in battle to survive and protect the region. The program is $15 from Zeta Software (P.O. Box 3522, Greenville, South Carolina 29608).

LUNAR LANDER. This program was published in the January/February, 1981 issue of *Sync* magazine. It was written in BASIC by Chuck Dawson. You must type this program into the computer before using it. You attempt to land your Lunar Lander on the surface of the moon by controlling the rate of final descent. If you descend too slowly you will use all of your fuel and crash. If you drop too quickly you will build up speed and crash land. Lots of luck!

HAMMURABI. Another BASIC program published in *Sync* magazine (January/February, 1981), this is a simulation that puts you in the role of a ruler of an ancient kingdom. You must make wise decisions or your kingdom will fall on hard times.

LIFE. A third BASIC program published in *Sync* magazine (March/April, 1981), this game simulates the life of an imaginary cellular life form. The details of LIFE were published in the October, 1970 and February, 1971 issues of *Scientific American* magazine.

SLOT MACHINE, ROULETTE, CRAPS, and BLACK-JACK. These programs cost $10 and come on a cassette. They are fairly good simulations of Las Vegas gambling games. They are available from Lamo-Lem Labs (Box 2382, La Jolla, California 92038).

SKI RUN. This BASIC program is one of several in a book called *The ZX81 Pocketbook* by Trevor Toms. It is published in England by Phipps Associates and in the U.S. by Reston. SKI RUN requires you to negotiate down a treacherous ski slope by pressing the correct keys on the computer's keyboard.

GROAN. This is one of the 32 programs in *32 BASIC Programs For the Timex Sinclair 1000* by Rugg, Feldman and Miller. It is a fast paced dice game. You play against the computer. There is a considerable amount of luck and some skill involved. The book is available from dilithium Press for $15.95 (P.O. Box E, Beaverton, Oregon 97075).

HOME AND SCHOOL APPLICATIONS

Like most small or personal computers the TS1000 can perform a variety of useful tasks in the home or school. A few of the things the computer can do are described below.

BYTE BACK MD-1. This is a $99 piece of equipment that lets you use your TS1000 to talk to other computers or computer networks over phone lines. The device is available from Byte-Back Co. (Rt. 3, Box 147, Brodie Road, Leesville, South Carolina 29070). Telecommunications is an exciting new area for small computers. For a complete description of all of the things you can do with a device like this you might want to read "Chapter 5, The Outer Limits: Communicating with the World," from *Computers for Everybody*, 2nd Ed.(dilithium Press, 1982).

CONSTELLATION. This $15 cassette program displays the night sky on your television screen. You can orient the display to simulate a view of the sky from different locations on earth. It is a useful educational program if you are interested in astronomy. The program comes from Gladstone Electronics (901 Fuhrman Blvd., Buffalo, New York 14203).

CHECKBOOK BALANCER/CALCULATOR. These are two of several programs available on cassette from Lamo-Lem (Box 2382, La Jolla, California 92038). The first program helps you balance your checkbook monthly. The second turns the computer into a high quality calculator. These programs are two of four on a cassette that costs $10.

ARITH-1.0. This BASIC program comes on a cassette. It will provide drill on addition and subtraction problems. It is $5 from Systems and Solutions, (5054 Kenerson Drive, Fairfax, Virginia 22032).

MULTIPLICATION THREE-IN-A-ROW. This is a BASIC program, written by Austin Brown, that was published in the July/August (1981) issue of *Sync* magazine. It is an adaptation of a program called "Multiplication Bingo." The computer displays a Tic Tac Toe grid with numbers in it. The user must answer multiplication problems in order to get an X in the square he or she selects. The goal is to get three Xs in a row before all the squares in the grid are used. It is a neat way to provide math drill while avoiding the boredom normally associated with such practice.

FRENCH VOCAB. Offered by a British company with the unlikely name of Bug-Byte (251 Henley Road, Coventry CV2 1BX England), the program requires extra memory and provides practice and testing on the English equivalents of 200 French words. Price is $19.

EXAM. This BASIC program is one of several in *The Sinclair ZX81*, a book by Randle Hurley. It is published by dilithium Press in the U.S. and by Macmillan Press in England. The program performs a variety of analyses on test scores which are typed into the computer. The book is about $12. dilithium Press also markets a cassette that contains all the programs listed in the book. The book and cassette together are about $20.

CASH. Another program from *The Sinclair ZX81*, this one helps you keep track of your family finances, the money coming in and out, where it goes, and what is due.

BUSINESS APPLICATIONS

The TS1000 is *not* a business computer. The computer was not designed for business applications, and in most situations it is likely to create more problems that it solves. You just cannot buy an adequate business computer for $99. That said, we must admit that a few brave souls do use the TS1000 in their businesses. Generally, the computer is used in very small businesses, and it does only one or two jobs. Larger, more expensive computers are capable of doing much more for the business owner and professional. Some of the business programs for the TS1000 are described below.

VU-CALC. This $30 cassette program does *some* of the same things the program VisiCalc does. VisiCalc is a $300 program that allows a business person to create and manipulate electronic spreadsheets. Mortgage tables, salary schedules, depreciation patterns, financial forecasts, job cost estimating, production scheduling, investment patterns, and mathematical tables are all easily created with an electronic spreadsheet. VU-CALC is a useful program, but does not have the power of spreadsheet programs such as VisiCalc and SuperCalc which run on computers with much larger memories. The program is available from Gladstone Electronics (see address above).

COMPUTACALC +. This is a $40 program similar to VU-CALC. You must add extra memory to your TS1000 in order to use this program. It is available from Mindware Co. (70 Boston Post Road, Wayland, Maryland 01778).

THE ESSENTIAL TIMEX/SINCLAIR

This computer, like most small computers, can be viewed as a system which is made up of several basic components. Figure 1.3 is a block diagram of the Timex Sinclair computer. Everything outside the dotted line, except the keyboard, you must supply yourself.

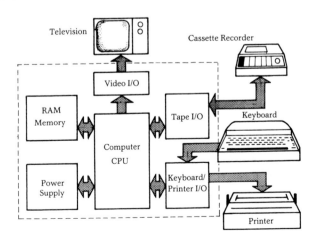

Figure 1.3 A block diagram of the TS1000.

The Power Supply

The TS1000 runs on 5 volt, direct current power. The black power supply unit shown in Figure 1.4 takes the 110 volts, alternating current, from your wall outlet and converts it to 9 volts. When you plug the power supply unit into the computer a voltage regulator inside it changes the 9 volts AC to 5 volts DC which is then routed to all the circuits on the board that need it. It is a simple power supply, but it does the job. Figure 1.5 shows the inside of the TS1000 with each major component labeled. The voltage regulator is in the upper left hand corner.

Figure 1.4 The power supply unit.

I/O Ports

I/O is an abbreviation for input/output. If a computer is to be of any use to you, it must be able to receive information and communicate its response back to you. This basic function is called Input/Output. The places on the computer circuit boards where I/O occurs are often called *ports*. The TS1000 is such a compact computer that most of the devices on its circuit boards do several jobs. The keyboard is your means of inputting information and instructions to the computer. It is soldered directly to the circuit board. When the TS1000 talks back to you it is usually via a television screen. It converts its messages to a video signal and sends them to the silver colored box at the top of the circuit board. That box is a video modulator. It converts the video signal to a signal your television can receive on a standard channel (either 2 or 3).

In addition to I/O ports for the keyboard and a television set, the TS1000 has provisions for connecting a tape recorder to it. A cable connects the earphone and microphone jacks on the recorder to I/O connectors on the computer board. The cassette

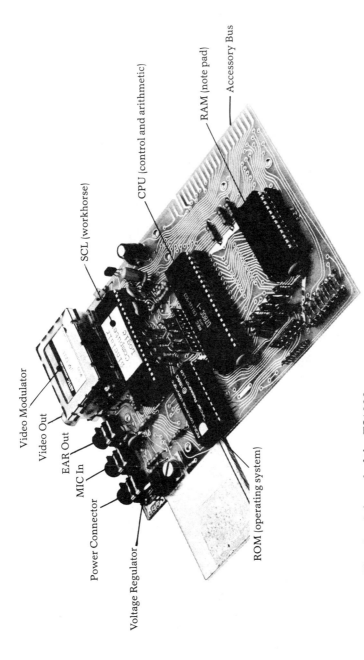

Figure 1.5 The circuit board of the TS1000.

I/O circuits allow you to store programs on a standard audio cassette tape and then "load" the program or data back into the computer when you want to use it again. A *program* is a set of instructions the computer follows to accomplish a particular task (e.g., balance your checkbook or play a game of chess). The computer then reads the instructions in a program and does what the instructions tell it to do. As you might expect, the instructions are not given orally. The TS1000 will not understand spoken instructions. The instructions are stored on the cassette in a code that is made up of a series of tones. If you listen to a tape, all you hear is a buzzing sound. That buzzing is music (instructions, actually) to the ear of the computer.

There is one more I/O port on the TS1000. It is the Accessory Bus which is located at the back of the computer on the right side. The Accessory Bus is actually a set of metal contacts at the edge of the board (bottom right of Figure 1.5). Each one of the little metal strips is connected to a particular circuit on the board. You can use the Accessory Bus to connect extra memory to your computer, to attach a printer, or to attach many of the other accessories that are available.

Memory

When you type something on the keyboard or load a program into the computer from a cassette, there must be somewhere to put that information. Each letter or number you type on the keyboard is converted to a code and stored in the memory of the computer. Each character you type in has its own code, a series of ones and zeros. A few of the codes are shown below:

keyboard character	internal code
A	0100110
B	0100111
1	0011101
2	0011110

All computers convert characters into codes of ones and zeros, but most do not use the TS1000 code. The code that is virtually a standard is called ASCII or American Standard Code for Information Interchange. Sinclair chose not to use ASCII and thus is different from almost every other small computer on the market. The principle, however, is the same. Each of the ones and zeros in the codes shown above is called a *bit*. Seven of those bits are used to define the code for each letter or character. Another bit, the eighth, is usually added to character code for purposes unrelated to our discussion here. Those eight bits are called a *byte*. Bytes are the fundamental code units for the TS1000 and most other computers. Memory inside the computer is also divided into bytes. One byte of memory can hold the electrical impulses that represent eight ones and zeros, or one byte.

Your computer contains two types of memory, *RAM* and *ROM*. ROM stands for Read Only Memory. This kind of memory is generally programmed at the factory. The contents of ROM cannot be changed by the user. The TS1000 ROM contains thousands of instructions for the computer. If there were no preprogrammed ROM in the computer you might have to give it instructions in patterns of ones and zeros, a fate we would not wish on anyone. Fortunately, when you plug the computer in, it automatically begins to follow the instructions in its ROM (the black integrated circuit on the middle left of Figure 1.5). Instead of ones and zeros, you can use English-like words in the BASIC computer language because the Sinclair programmers wrote instructions for the computer that let you do that.

All computer memory cannot be ROM, however. Much of the memory in the TS1000 is RAM, or Random Access Memory. The standard ZX81 has a little over 1000 bytes of RAM, the Timex 1000 has a little over 2000. Since each byte contains one character of information, the 1000 byte memory stores up to 1000 characters. RAM is also known as *volatile* memory. It is general-purpose memory. You can store data or instructions in RAM, tell the computer to use the information you've stored there, and then replace the material in RAM with something new. You can put data in RAM (write to memory) and you can take it out (read from memory). You can only read ROM. The biggest problem with RAM is the fact that whatever is in it disappears when the computer is turned off. If you need to save something in RAM for use later, it is necessary to store it on a cassette before turning the computer off. Material in ROM remains there forever. The standard RAM in the TS1000 is the black IC (integrated circuit) at the bottom of Figure 1.5. Several companies, including Timex and Sinclair, sell extra RAM memory for the computer. You will see ads for "16K RAM" and for "64K RAM." Memory is often referred to in terms of "K." Each K of memory is 1024 bytes. Thus 16K would be 1024 times 16 or 16384 bytes. Similarly, 64K of RAM would be 1024 times 64 or 65536 bytes. That is quite a bit more than the 1024 bytes contained in the standard ZX81.

CHAPTER 2

Setup and Installation

Even the basic TS1000 computer comes with accessories. There is the power supply, the cable that connects the television to the computer, a switch box that lets you switch between regular TV reception and the computer display, and the cable needed to attach the computer to a cassette recorder. This chapter will show you how to connect everything together and how to adjust the television set.

CONNECTING THE COMPUTER TO THE TELEVISION

The TS1000 produces a signal that ordinary televisions can receive on either channel 2 or 3. There is a switch on the bottom of the computer that lets you select which channel you want to use. If your city does not have a television station on channel 2 or 3, the switch can be set to either 2 or 3. It should work fine on either one. If you have a Channel 2 or 3 in your area use the switch to select an unused channel to minimize the chances of interference. If you have channels on both 2 and 3 use the one with the weaker station for the computer. NOTE: Although the great majority of TS1000 computers sold in the United States use Channel 2 or 3 some units in the U.S. and many sold elsewhere in the world may not have the switch on the bottom of the case and/or they may not use Channel 2 or 3. Some units, in fact, use a UHF channel (e.g., 32) rather than a VHF channel. European models of the TS1000 have a different design since European televisions are not compatible with American and Canadian television sets. Check the manual that came with your computer to determine which channel to use. Since we assume you have a standard Channel 2-3 model in the instructions below, you will want to adjust the directions if you do not.

Figure 2.1 The channel selector switch on the bottom of the computer.

The TS1000 works best on a black and white television. It can be connected to a color television as well, but the display will still be in black and white. In addition, we have had more difficulty getting a clear, clean display on color televisions. Even some black and white televisions do not work well with the computer. In addition to the signal it intends to send to the television, the TS1000 can also generate quite a bit of electronic "noise" that can show up in your picture as interference. Some televisions are more resistant to interference than others. If you cannot get a good display, try moving the cable around that connects the computer to the television. Then try another television. If you plan to buy a small television to use with the TS1000 it would be advisable to take the computer to the store and try it out with the particular model you plan to buy before making the purchase (or get the store to agree that you can return it if it doesn't work well).

Attach the TV switch box to the VHF connector on the back of the television (see Figure 2.2). If you have an antenna lead or cable line connected to the VHF terminal, remove it and attach

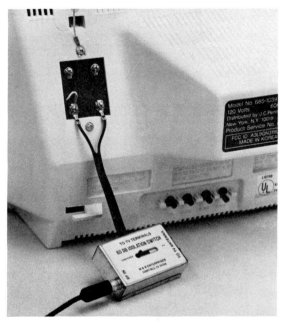

Figure 2.2 Connecting the computer to your television.

it to the switch box. Use the terminals marked "antenna" (see Figure 2.3). Now, take the video cable (about 4 feet long) that came with the computer and connect one end to the switch box (this cable has RCA type phone plug connectors on each end). Connect the other end of the cable to the TV jack on the left back side of the computer (see Figure 2.4).

With the television connected you can now use the slide switch lever on the switch box to select the signal from the computer or from the antenna/cable lead. Set the switch box at the back of the television to "computer" for now. Since the box has two sided tape attached to it, you can peel the protective paper off the tape and attach the box permanently to the back or side of the TV if you wish. Press hard for a good bond and be

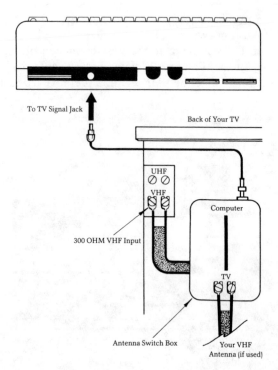

To TV Signal Jack

Back of Your TV

UHF

VHF

Computer

300 OHM VHF Input

TV

Antenna Switch Box

Your VHF
Antenna (if used)

Figure 2.3 A diagram of the connections used to hook up the
TS1000.

Figure 2.4 Connecting the video cable to the connector at the
side of the TS1000.

sure the box is located where you want it before pressing because it is hard to remove and relocate.

THE TAPE RECORDER CONNECTIONS

It is not absolutely necessary to connect a tape recorder now, but if you plan to load taped programs into the computer's memory or save programs on tape, you might as well set it up now.

Find the cassette recorder cable shown in Figure 2.5. It has miniature phone plug jacks on both ends of a grey and a black cable. Your tape recorder should have a jack on it labeled EAR or OUT or something similar. Plug the grey cable into that jack on the recorder. Now plug the other end of the grey cable into the jack labeled EAR on the left side of the computer (see Figure 2.5). The EAR to EAR connection will allow the computer to listen to signals from the recorder.

There should also be a jack labeled MIC on the recorder. Plug one end of the black cable into it and plug the other end into the jack labeled MIC on the computer. The MIC to MIC connection will allow the computer to send signals to the recorder. Although we told you to use the grey cable for the EAR connection and the black one for MIC, it really doesn't make any difference as long as you don't get the cables crossed.

If you have a standard cassette recorder it is likely to work with the TS1000. If you purchase one especially for use with the computer look for one with the following characteristics:

Figure 2.5 The cassette recorder to computer connections.

1. Fast forward and fast reverse controls that lock down when pressed. They are more convenient.

2. An accurate counter, conveniently located. If you put more than one program on a tape, the counter will help you locate each one.

3. Tone control. Adjusting the tone may enable you to load some tapes that otherwise could not be loaded.

4. AC power. If you get a hum on your tapes when you try to save a program it may be necessary to run the recorder on batteries. The hum may be 60 cycle hum picked up from your house current. In most instances, however, battery operation is to be avoided because the motor speed changes as the batteries get weaker.

5. A meter that indicates the volume level when recording or playing back. Tapes recorded and played back at a certain volume level work better than those recorded at other levels. If you have a working meter on your recorder you can find the best level by trial and error and then adjust the volume control so that you are always recording or playing back at the best volume level. (You can't just set the volume control and leave it there since the same setting doesn't produce the same volume on every tape.)

In terms of cassettes, we have found most of the name brand tapes to be reliable. AVOID the four-for-a-$1 specials, however. They are generally of poor quality and can create reliability problems. It is difficult to get the computer to record and playback programs consistently with good quality equipment and tapes; it is almost impossible with tapes that are seconds or that were shoddily manufactured. We pay between $1.25 and $3.75 for the tapes we use (C30s to C60s).

THE POWER CONNECTION

There is one more cable to be attached. Plug the black power supply into a convenient wall outlet. Then plug the end with the miniature phone plug jack into the jack labeled 9VDC on the left side of the computer. Be sure to plug the TV and the cassette player into a wall outlet too. That's it! You are in business.

TAKE IT FOR A SPIN

All the connections have now been made. In fact, the computer is already working since you plugged in the power sup-

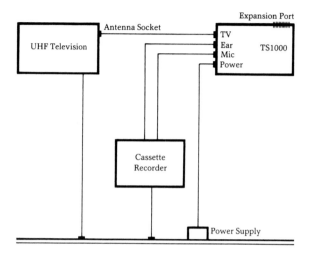

Figure 2.6 Connections for the TS1000.

ply. Turn on the television and look for a screen that looks like Figure 2.7. Set the channel selector to the same channel as the computer (i.e., either 2 or 3 on most TS1000s). The only thing you should see on the screen is a small white K surrounded by a square of black. It will be near the bottom of the screen on the left side.

Figure 2.7 Initial video display.

Unless you have a very good television the K is likely to be somewhat fuzzy. You may not even be able to tell what it is. Use the fine tune control and the brightness/contrast controls to get as legible a display as possible. If you get something else on the screen, or nothing, pull the power connector out of the 9VDC jack on the computer, wait a few seconds, and insert it again. You should get the K now. If you don't, check all your connections. Are they correct? Turn up the volume on the television and unplug the power to the computer again. When you plug it back in, does the sound of the TV change? If it does that indicates the computer is operating. If all else fails try another TV. When you get your K move on to Chapter 3. Happy computing!

CHAPTER 3

How to Get Your Computer Up and Running

At this point you should have all your cables correctly connected with the computer and the television plugged in. You may have noted that there is no On/Off switch on the computer. The only way you can switch it on and off is by unplugging the power cord. That cord should be plugged in now and the television turned on. You should see a K in the bottom left corner of the television screen. If there is no K, or if the screen has a lot of interference on it, return to Chapter 2 for instructions and suggestions. At this point we assume that there is a K on the screen and you are ready to go.

THE KEYBOARD/DISPLAY CONNECTION

The primary way you will interact with your computer is by typing in information on its keyboard. The primary way it will communicate with you is via the television screen.

The keyboard on the TS1000 uses the QWERTY layout found on standard typewriters. That is, the top row of letters begins with Q on the left and has WERTYUIOP across. Figure 3.1 is an illustration of the keyboard. If you touch type, the location of letters and numbers will be familiar to you. This is not, however, a standard typewriter-style keyboard. It is a membrane keyboard that is less than half the size of an IBM Selectric keyboard. The keyboard will feel quite different from a typewriter. The keys don't snap as you press a letter. The feel is more of a mush than a snap. In the beginning you probably won't be able to feel when you have pressed the key hard enough to register a response; looking at the display will be the only way to tell what you have accomplished. Pressing straight down in the center of each keypad seems to work best. When you press a keypad you press on a "sandwich" of two conductive pieces of plastic with some spongy material between them. If you push hard enough, all the spongy insulation is squeezed out of the way and contact is made.

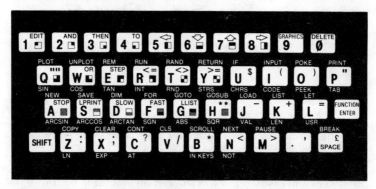

Figure 3.1 The TS1000 keyboard.

The keyboard may be small, but it is very busy. Look at the P keypad. Like most keypads there is a letter printed in the middle. There is also a symbol printed in red, a word printed above the white keypad, and a word printed below it. This one keypad has four different functions depending on when you press it and whether you press the SHIFT key at the same time. Some of the keys have five different functions. Consider R. There is a graphics symbol right beside the R, a less than or equal to symbol in red, the word RUN above, and the abbreviation INT (for Integer) below. As we said, this is a busy keyboard. Depending on when and how you press the R key you may cause any of the following to appear on the screen:

>   R
>   < =
>   RUN
>   INT
>   a small square, three fourths black

YOUR FIRST PROGRAM

Let's try a little work with the keyboard. With everything plugged in and turned on (and the K on the screen), press the following keys:

10 (be sure and press the number 1, not the capital I, and the number 0, not the letter O).

When you press the 1 key the number one should appear on the screen. After the 0 is pressed, the number ten should be displayed at the bottom of the screen. The little white-on-black K should be just in front of the 10. Now press the following keys:

I N (SHIFT)U **ENTER**

The line above means, press the letter I, then press N, then hold the SHIFT key down and press U; press the ENTER key. When you press the I key, the word **INPUT** should appear on the screen. **INPUT** is a keyword, and the white-on-black K tells you that if you press a key that has a key word above it, that key word will be printed. (You did not get a key word when you pressed the 1 and 0 keys because there is no key word above those key pads.) After **INPUT** was displayed the inverse letter (the white-on-black letter) changed from a K to an L. The inverse L lets you know that the computer is no longer looking for a key word. L stands for *literal*. With it you get the letter or number shown on the key. When you pressed the N key, the letter N appeared. Finally, pressing the SHIFT and U key produced the dollar sign ($) symbol. On a normal keyboard, a shifted letter would produce the capital of that letter. On the TS1000 keyboard, capital letters are all you get. There are no lowercase characters. The SHIFT key is used to get the symbols and punctuation marks that are shown in red on the keyboard.

Something new should have happened when you pressed the ENTER key. The line of instructions you just typed (10 **INPUT** N$) was placed at the top of the screen. Pressing ENTER told the computer you were finished with line 10. The computer put it at the top of the screen and made room for another line at the bottom of the screen.

If You Make a Mistake

Unless you are a much better typist that most of us, you will make some errors as you type in this first program. There are several things you can do to correct errors.

BEFORE PRESSING ENTER. If you spot an error before pressing the ENTER key, you can use the RIGHT ARROW and LEFT ARROW keys to move the cursor around on the line you are writing. The *cursor* is the inverse-K or L that tells you where you are on the line. (The RIGHT ARROW and LEFT ARROW keys are actually (SHIFT) 5 and (SHIFT) 8.) Each time you press one of the arrow keys, the cursor moves in the direction of the arrow. If you use the arrow keys to place the cursor over a letter or symbol on the line, any letters or symbols you type will be inserted at that point in the line. Everything to the right of the cursor will be pushed over to make room. This insert feature allows you to add material where needed. That is one way of correcting an error.

Another means of correcting an error is with the DELETE key (actually SHIFT 0). Each time you press the DELETE key the letter or symbol to the left of the cursor is deleted from the line. Even the space it occupied is gone. The computer moves material to the right into the space. When you use the arrow keys to move over a key word such as **PRINT** or **INPUT** the cursor jumps over the entire key word at once. You cannot move the cursor across each letter of the key word. If you press the DELETE key while the cursor is just to the right of a key word you will delete the entire key word. For example pressing DELETE while the cursor is in the space to the right of **INPUT** would delete **INPUT** rather than just the T.

AFTER PRESSING ENTER. Often you will not notice an error until you have already pressed the ENTER key and the line has been placed at the top of the screen. Again there are several things you can do.

The S cursor. The TS1000 checks each line you type in before putting it at the top of the screen. If it finds an error, it will not let you enter the line. Instead, it keeps the line at the bottom of the screen and places an inverse S cursor just to the left of the point where the first error occurs in the line. This is a feature found on very few computers, but it is an excellent idea. You can use the arrow keys and the DELETE key to correct the error. It may take some effort to figure out why the TS1000 rejected your line.

No S cursor. The computer will not catch every error. Some will slip through, and you will find them after the line appears at the top of the screen. You have several options. If you retype the line correctly and press ENTER, the new version of the line will replace the old one. That is the simplest thing to do. If you accidentally type in a line that shouldn't be there at all, just type the number of the line and press ENTER. That will cause the entire line to be deleted from the screen. For example, if you accidentally put a line 99 into the program, typing 99 and pressing ENTER will delete the line entirely. There is another process called *editing* a line that we will deal with later. You can correct any mistakes you make, however, with the methods described above.

Now type in the following:

20 P N (SHIFT)U (SHIFT)X (SHIFT)P SPACE CAN YOU PROGRAM ME (SHIFT)C (SHIFT)P ENTER

The line above directs you to press the P key, the N key, then a shifted U, a shifted X, and shifted P, the space key, type in the phrase CAN YOU PROGRAM ME, a shifted C, a shifted P, and the ENTER key. For all that effort you should see the following at the top of the screen:

20 **PRINT** N$;" CAN YOU PROGRAM ME?"

Since this line is too long to fit on one line the last part (ME?") will be on a separate line. It was necessary to use the shift key to get symbols such as the dollar sign (SHIFT U), and punctuation marks such as the semicolon (SHIFT X), the question mark (SHIFT C), and quotation marks (SHIFT P). From now on we won't show you how to get those symbols and punctuation marks. If you need a symbol or punctuation mark that is printed in red (e.g., a plus sign) just hold the SHIFT key down and press the correct keypad (e.g., K). In addition, we will spell out the key word in each line. Just remember that words such as PRINT, INPUT, and DIM should not be typed in letter by letter. Just press the key with that word above it. Key words will be printed in bold type in this book. Read the note below and then type in the following lines:

30 **INPUT** A$
40 **IF** A$ = "YES" **THEN** GOTO 100
50 **IF** A$ = "NO" **THEN** GOTO 110
100 **PRINT** "GREAT, WE WILL HAVE FUN."
105 **GOTO** 200
110 **PRINT** "NOT TO WORRY, YOU WILL LEARN."
200 **REM** END OF PROGRAM
  5 **PRINT** "HELLO WHAT IS YOUR NAME?"

Note: Lines 40 and 50 use a special instruction — IF THEN. Typing these lines is a little complicated. First, type the beginning number as usual (i.e., 40) then press the U key to get the **IF** key word. You now have an inverse-L cursor. Type A (SHIFT)U (SHIFT)L (SHIFT)P YES (SHIFT)P. That should produce the following:

40 **IF** A$ = "YES"

That is the first part of line 40. You have an inverse-L cursor which means you can't get key words just by pressing a letter. The key word you need next, however, is **THEN**. It is a red word on the 3 key. Hold the SHIFT key down and press the 3 key. That puts **THEN** on the screen, and you now have an inverse-K cursor. Press the G key and you get **GOTO**. Finally, type in 100 and press ENTER. The following line should now be added to your program at the top of the screen:

40 **IF** A$ = "YES" **THEN** GOTO 100

Use the same procedure to type in line 50. Just remember you can't get a regular key word (word in white above the key) when the cursor is an inverse-L. Key words in red however, can be obtained by pressing the SHIFT key and the correct letter key.

Another Note: When you type in line 5 and press ENTER, the computer places line 5 at the beginning of the program, in its correct numerical position, and not after line 200. The TS1000 will arrange your lines numerically regardless of the order in which you type them.

YOU HAVE A PROGRAM!

At this point you have your first program in the computer. The material at the top of the screen should look like this:

```
 5 PRINT "HELLO WHAT IS YOUR NAME?"
10 INPUT N$
20 PRINT N$;" CAN YOU PROGRAM ME?"
30 INPUT A$
40 IF A$ = "YES" THEN GOTO 100
50 IF A$ = "NO" THEN GOTO 110
100 PRINT "GREAT, WE WILL HAVE FUN."
```

105 **GOTO** 200
110 **PRINT** "NOT TO WORRY, YOU WILL LEARN."
200 **REM** END OF PROGRAM

Lines 20, 100, and 110 are too long to be displayed on one line on your screen and line 200 will probably have a white greater than sign displayed in a black square between the number 200 and the key word **REM**. We will deal with the inverse-greater than symbol later.

The material you have just typed in is a computer program which was written in BASIC, a very popular computer language. The TS1000 uses a relatively powerful dialect of BASIC which has much in common with the versions of BASIC used by other personal computers such as the Apple II, Atari 800, Commodore VIC, and the Radio Shack computers.

A program is a set of instructions you want the computer to follow. The instructions are organized into lines, and each line begins with a line number. When the computer is told to follow or *execute* the instructions in a program it begins with the instructions in the line with the smallest number. It executes the instructions in that line first; then it moves on to the line with the next smallest number and executes the instructions there. It thus moves sequentially through the program, from lowest line number to highest line number. If you do not want the computer to follow this standard or *default* pattern it is necessary to tell the computer what line you want it to do next. If you don't, it will move sequentially through the program.

How do you get the computer to execute your program? It is really very simple. The BASIC in the TS1000 uses the key word **RUN** to tell the computer to follow the instructions in a program you typed in or one you have loaded into the computer from cassette. **RUN** is the key word over the R key. Press R and **RUN** should appear in the bottom left corner of the screen. Now press the ENTER key. The screen should be clear except for an inverse-L in the bottom left corner. Press ENTER again and the program will begin execution. The sentence HELLO, WHAT IS YOUR NAME? appears at the top of the screen. Type in your first name and press ENTER. If you type in JERRY and press ENTER the computer will reply, JERRY, CAN YOU PROGRAM ME? Type in either YES or NO. Let's say you type in NO. Press ENTER. The computer should respond NOT TO WORRY, YOU WILL LEARN.

You have now typed in a program and it has been **RUN**. If it didn't work as expected look back over the lines you typed in and try to find the problem. For example, if the number 0 was typed for the letter O in line 50 the program won't work correctly when you type NO. When the program runs correctly read the explanation of each line in the section that follows.

A Line By Line Explanation of the Program

Chapters 6 and 7 deal with the BASIC language used by the TS1000 in some detail. This section will explain what happens as each line of your first program is executed.

5 **PRINT** "HELLO, WHAT IS YOUR NAME?"

This line contains the key word **PRINT** and the sentence HELLO, WHAT IS YOUR NAME? The key word **PRINT** instructs the computer to print whatever appears on the line just after **PRINT**. The quotation marks before and after the sentence tell the computer to print the material just as it appears in the program.

10 **INPUT** N$

The key word **INPUT** tells the computer to look for something to be typed in on the keyboard. If you type in AMY and press ENTER the computer sets aside a section of its memory and puts the characters AMY there. It then makes N$ equal to AMY. N$ is a "variable name" and AMY is the content of that variable. Later in the program if you tell the computer to **PRINT** N$ the computer will print AMY rather than N$. On the other hand, if you tell the computer to **PRINT** "N$" the computer would actually print N$ because you enclosed it in quotation marks.

20 **PRINT** N$;" CAN YOU PROGRAM ME?"

The key word again is **PRINT**. Since N$ is not enclosed in quotation marks the computer checks to see what N$ stands for. If it is AMY, that is what is printed on the screen. The semicolon tells the computer to print whatever follows right next to the material that was just printed. The rest of the sentence is between quotation marks so it will be printed as is. Thus the sentence AMY CAN YOU PROGRAM ME? will appear on the screen.

30 **INPUT** A$

This line is just like line 10 except that whatever you type in will be assigned the variable name A$ rather than N$. We chose the letter A because this is an answer to a question. The N in N$ is short for name.

40 **IF** A$ = "YES" **THEN GOTO** 100

There are three key words in this line: **IF**, **THEN**, and **GOTO**. The line tells the computer to check what A$ stands for. If A$ stands for YES then the instruction after **THEN** is executed. In line 40 the key word **GOTO** instructs the computer to skip to line 100 and begin executing the instructions there **IF** and only if A$ equals YES.

50 **IF** A$ = "NO" **THEN GOTO** 110

This line, like line 40 tells the computer to check what A$ equals. If A$ equals NO the computer jumps to line 110 for instructions. If A$ equals YES, the computer never reads or executes the instructions in line 50 since it jumps from line 40 to line 100. If A$ equals NO the computer never reads or executes the instructions in lines 100 and 105 since it jumps from 50 to 110.

100 **PRINT** "GREAT, WE WILL HAVE FUN."

The key word in line 100 is **PRINT**. The line causes the sentence in quotation marks to be printed on your screen.

105 **GOTO** 200

If A$ equals YES and line 100 prints its cheery comment, the program has accomplished its purpose. You don't want the other comment in line 110 to be printed so **GOTO** 200 sends the computer from line 105 to line 200.

110 **PRINT** "NOT TO WORRY, YOU WILL LEARN."

If A$ equals NO the computer jumps from line 50 to line 110 where an encouraging comment is printed on the screen.

200 **REM** END OF PROGRAM

The key word **REM** is short for REMARK. **REM** tells the computer to ignore anything else that is typed after **REM**. **REM** instructions are very important because they let you

write comments or messages to yourself or to other people who
may be using the program. The example program is short and
does not require **REM** lines for clarity. Longer programs
should have **REM** lines sprinkled liberally throughout, with
messages that explain what each section of the program does.
That makes it easier to work with the program months or years
after you wrote it, and **REM** lines make it easier for others to
modify or adapt your program to their own needs.

When the computer reaches line 200 it cannot find another
line of instruction to execute. It stops and waits for you to tell it
what to do next. The 0/200 in the bottom left corner of the
screen tells you the last line read and executed by the computer
(200). The 0 tells you that no errors were found. The meaning of
other numbers you may find lurking in that corner of the
screen will be discussed in Chapters 6 and 7. Press the ENTER
key again and the 0/200 should change to an inverse-K. That
means you are back to the key word mode.

At this point you may be thinking that this example program
was too simple, that writing programs for a computer is far
more complicated than this. It is true that there are some key
words that are more difficult to understand than the ones used
so far. And there are complex, sophisticated procedures used
by professional programmers that can't be picked up easily in a
weekend while keeping one eye on the football games. But,
having said all that, it is also true that you can quickly and
easily learn to write your own programs in a language like
BASIC. The skills you learn are some of the same ones used by
programmers who spend most of their waking hours at the
keyboard of a computer. In addition, if you learn the key words
in BASIC and how programs are written, you will be able to use
programs you find in magazines on your own computer, and
you will be able to adapt and personalize programs. The final
section of this chapter presents one more BASIC program that
illustrates one of the nicer features of the TS1000, graphics.
There are a number of good BASIC programming books available that will help you expand your programming ability. A
good one is *Instant Freeze Dried Computer Programming In
BASIC 2nd Astounding Edition* (dilithium Press).

GRAPHICS AND THE TS1000

The TS1000 computer can display a number of graphics
characters as well as letters, numbers, and symbols. Those

graphics symbols are shown on the keyboard in red just below the words or symbols. If you have a program in the computer's memory now, press the A key while you have an inverse-K cursor. That should put **NEW** on the screen. Press ENTER and the program in memory will be completely erased. If a key word such as **NEW** is typed on the screen without a line number in front of it, the key word is executed as soon as you press ENTER. There is no need to tell the computer to run the instruction.

Now you're ready to type in another program. You should have a blank screen with an inverse-K cursor at the bottom.

Type in the following program (see comments after the program before entering it into the computer):

```
10 FOR X = 1 TO 4
20 PRINT "■ ■■■";
30 PRINT " ◳◳ ◳◳";
40 NEXT X
50 REM END OF PROGRAM
```

This program can be typed in like the first one. That is, key words like **FOR**, **PRINT**, and **NEXT** are entered by pressing one key. When you type in line 10, note that the key word **TO** is not above a key. It is written in red on the 4 key. That means you will have to hold the SHIFT key down and press 4 to get **TO**.

Lines 20 and 30 use graphics symbols and are a bit tricky to get correctly. Here is a step-by-step guide for line 20:

1. Press the 2 and the 0 keys.
2. Press the P key. (**PRINT** should appear on the screen.)
3. Hold down the SHIFT key and press P. (That should produce a ".)
4. Now you want to type in four of the graphics symbols shown on the H key. In order to use a graphics symbol you must first get into the graphics mode. Hold down the SHIFT key and press the 9. The cursor will change to an inverse-G which indicates you are now in graphics mode.
5. Hold down the SHIFT key and press the H key four times. That should put four graphics symbols on the screen.
6. You are finished with graphics for the moment so hold down SHIFT and press 9 again. That gets you out of graphics mode. The inverse-G cursor changes back to an inverse-L.

7. Hold down SHIFT and press P. That should give you ending quotation marks.
8. You need a semicolon so hold down SHIFT and press X.
9. Finally, press the ENTER key. Line 30 is typed in the same way. Just remember that you must get into the graphics mode (SHIFT 9) to get the graphics symbols and you must then get out of graphics mode (SHIFT 9 again) to return to normal operation. If you forget to get out of the graphics mode letters you press will show up white on a dark background (inverse). You won't be able to type in a key word while in the graphics mode.

When you've finished typing in the program, check it carefully for errors. Then RUN the program (press R then ENTER). The program creates a pattern of grey and checkered rectangles across the top of the screen. It is possible to use over 20 different graphics symbols to create anything from a chessboard to a business chart on the screen. The details of graphics on the TS1000 will be given in a later chapter.

A SECTION BY SECTION EXPLANATION OF THE PROGRAM.

10 **FOR** X = 1 **TO** 4

The key word **FOR** in line 10 is a handy one. When the computer reads the word **FOR** it looks at the next letter (X in this line) and at the value initially assigned to that letter (1 in this case). **FOR** is matched with another key word, **NEXT**. The computer will move on from line 10 to lines 20 and 30. It executes the instructions found there. When it gets to line 40 it finds a **NEXT** X instruction. That is a signal for the computer to go back to the line where **FOR** occurs (line 10 in this program). Before going back to line 10, however, the computer adds 1 to the value of X. In fact, the computer adds 1 to the value of X each time it loops through the instructions from line 10 to line 40. When the value of X equals the second number on line 10 (4), the computer stops looping back from 40 to 10. Instead it goes on to line 50 which is the end of the program.

20 **PRINT** "■■ ■■";

This line puts a series of four grey shaded graphics symbols on the screen. In addition, the semicolon at the end of the line tells the computer to put the next item to be printed right after the four graphics symbols. If the semicolon were omitted, the next **PRINT** instruction would begin printing on the line below the one used by **PRINT** in line 20.

30 **PRINT** "🞔🞔 🞔🞔";

Line 30 works just like line 20. Four graphics symbols are displayed on the top line of the video screen, just after the ones printed by line 20. Since a semicolon comes right after the material to be printed, the next **PRINT** instruction will start its work right after 🞔🞔 🞔🞔 on the top line of the screen.

40 **NEXT** X

The **NEXT** instruction is the lower boundary of the loop. A loop consists of those instructions between a **FOR** and a **NEXT** instruction. In this program the **FOR** instruction in line 10 tells the computer to execute the instructions inside the loop four times. **NEXT** defines the end of that loop. Thus, the first time the computer goes through the loop you get:

■■ ■■🞔🞔🞔🞔

The next time the computer goes through the loop, you have:

■ ■ ■■🞔🞔🞔🞔■ ■■■ 🞔🞔🞔🞔

After the third execution of the loop, the screen displays:

■■■■🞔🞔🞔🞔■ ■■■🞔🞔🞔🞔■■ ■■■🞔🞔🞔🞔

Finally, the fourth and last execution of the loop produces:

■■ ■■🞔🞔🞔🞔■■■ ■■🞔🞔🞔🞔■■ ■■🞔🞔🞔🞔■■ ■■🞔🞔🞔🞔

After the fourth time through the loop the computer moves on to the next instruction in the program.

50 **REM** END OF PROGRAM

This final line in the program is a **REM** (remark) line. It carries a message the programmer can read, but the computer ignores it. The program ends with line 50 and the screen contains a checkered line at the top.

One line of graphics isn't really something to write home about, but the TS1000 is capable of creating all sorts of displays on your screen. Many of the programs for the TS1000 in magazines like *Sync* and *Syntax Quarterly* (see Chapter 10 for information on these and other magazines) use the graphics features of this computer to create all sorts of interesting effects.

CHAPTER 4

Loading Programs into the Computer

When engineers first thought of designing a personal computer that would be inexpensive enough to be purchased and used by individuals, they had to deal with the issue of mass storage or permanent storage. If you type a program into the memory of the computer it will remain there as long as the computer is on. Switch the computer off (or use the **NEW** key word) and the program in the computer's memory is gone forever. To be truly useful, the computer must have some means of storing programs for use later. In addition, there must be some way for programmers to mass produce the programs they wish to sell to owners of personal computers.

Virtually all the small, inexpensive personal computers sold today use conventional audio cassette tape systems to store programs. Cassette storage is cheap and easy to use. Programs and data are stored on the cassette as a series of tones. When you buy a program for your TS1000 it is likely to be stored on a cassette. To use it, you must tell the computer to listen to the pattern of tones recorded on the cassette and convert them to data that will be placed in RAM. If you plan to buy a cassette recorder for use with the TS1000 a list of desirable recorder features is presented in Chapter 2.

The cassette tape solution, unfortunately, has only one advantage (it is cheap) and many disadvantages. It is slow and often unreliable. A large program can take as long as ten minutes or more to be transferred from tape into the memory of the computer. That may not seem like a long time now, but when you're in front of the computer waiting it can seem like forever.

MAKING THE CONNECTIONS

Before information can be transferred from your cassette tape to the computer, all the various plugs and wires must be properly connected to each piece of equipment. See Chapter 2 for detailed information on how to connect the computer to the TV. Figure 4.1 shows the computer already connected to the TV. Notice that there is a cable that has two jacks on each end, one black and one grey. This is the recorder cable. On the left side of the computer are two outlets, one labeled EAR and one labeled MIC. Your recorder should also have two outlets; one

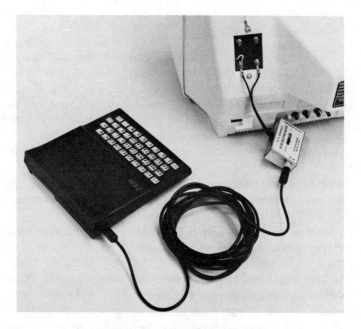

Figure 4.1 The TS1000 connected to a television.

may be labeled EAR or OUT (or something similar) and one labeled MIC. Plug one of the grey cables into the EAR outlet on the computer. Plug the grey cable on the other end into the EAR outlet on the recorder (see Figure 4.2). This connection allows the computer to listen to signals from the cassette recorder. Now, plug one of the black cables into the connection marked MIC on the computer. The black jack on the other end goes to the MIC outlet on the recorder. This allows the computer to "talk" or send signals to the recorder.

Although we suggested that you use the grey cables for the EAR connection and the black ones for MIC, it doesn't make any difference which is used. The crucial element is to make certain that the cable (grey or black) connected to EAR on the tape recorder is the same cable connected to EAR on the computer. The same applies to the MIC connection.

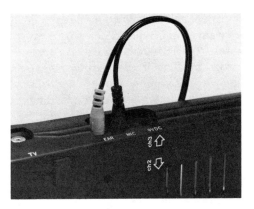

Figure 4.2 The ear connections.

Figure 4.3 Proper connections.

GET READY FOR PROBLEMS

When the computer is connected to the power, a fuzzy K will appear at the bottom left side of the TV screen. You may need to adjust the brightness and contrast on your set until the K is obvious.

Once there is a K on the TV screen, you are ready to put programs into your TS1000. The process of getting those programs from a cassette tape into the memory of the computer is called *loading*. The reverse, storing data from the computer's memory on a tape is called *saving*. This chapter deals with how to **LOAD** programs and Chapter 5 describes how to **SAVE**.

Unfortunately, the TS1000 has a deservedly bad reputation for loading programs. That is, the computer is extremely particular about the way the volume and tone controls are set on the tape recorder. What happens during the loading process? Programs or data stored on the cassette tape are "read" into the computer's memory. You may want to disconnect the EAR jack from the tape recorder and listen to a program. It sounds like a lot of interference to the human ear, but not to the computer. There is a pattern to the noise that the computer can translate. The pattern of noise must be at a specific volume and tone level or the computer cannot decode it. Therefore, these settings are crucial. If either setting is off a fraction, the pattern is wrong, the computer doesn't understand, and the program doesn't **LOAD**. (Remember to plug the EAR jack back into the recorder.)

It is recommended that you turn the tone control (if you have one on your recorder) to the highest setting and leave it there. That worked well for us. Once that was done, the tone setting rarely caused any problems.

The culprit in most loading problems seems to be volume control. There is a narrow range that the computer can tolerate. We have a Radio Shack CTR-80A cassette recorder that we use with the TS1000. At first the volume setting that worked was between 4 and 6 (there isn't a 5 marked on this model). For several weeks of loading programs from one tape, this setting was consistent. If (in spite of our warnings) someone changed the volume control, we could set it back to between 4 and 6 and it worked fine. Then one day, two of the programs on our favorite tape wouldn't **LOAD**. We checked the volume and it was at the usual setting. The tone control was at the proper setting too. Our next fear was that something was wrong with the tape. Before giving up, however, we decided to try changing the volume. We could tell by the TV display that part of the program was being read (we'll explain what the screen looks like when things are going right later in this chapter). We slowly increased the volume to 6 and sure enough, the program loaded. For some reason (the tape may be worn or there may be a problem with our recorder) those two programs will not **LOAD** now, except at the higher levels. The other programs on the tape will not **LOAD** at the 6 level, however; they have to be loaded with the volume set at between 4 and 5 and a half. Loading programs into the TS1000, is unfortunately, more of an art than a science. You will have to practice with the computer and the particular model of recorder you are using in order to get the feel of how it works.

The TS1000 is not the only computer that has this problem. Any computer that relies on a tape recorder for input is likely to be troublesome, but the TS1000 is probably one of the most difficult. There may be times when programs **LOAD** with no problem at all. Then there will be times when nothing seems to go right. In short, be prepared to try the loading instructions several times. The directions and suggestions we give are based on hours of experience. Some of the hours were happy ones. Some were, well, frustrating at best. The major contributing factor to problems is the volume setting. Turn this setting up or down in small increments until you hit the perfect setting. In addition, it is suggested that you choose a short program for determining the best volume setting. Waiting for a four or five minute program to **LOAD**, only to find it doesn't, is time consuming and frustrating. A shorter program reduces the time spent in waiting and makes the task a little less aggravating.

LOADing Steps

Suppose you want to **LOAD** a program called SUM. (If you don't have a program to **LOAD**, read Chapter 5 on how to **SAVE** programs before proceeding.) After the computer is connected to the TV and cassette recorder, and the K is located in the lower left corner of the TV screen, follow these steps to load the program:

1. Turn the tone control to its highest level.
2. Insert the cassette into the recorder.

3. Make certain the cassette is rewound to a point a little before the actual beginning of the program. Starting the recorder at the very beginning of a program may result in some information being lost. It is a good idea to use a recorder that has a tape counter. This feature allows you to keep track of where a program begins and ends and thus can save you time in searching for a program.

4. Press the J key. Notice that above the letter J is the word **LOAD**. **LOAD** appears on the screen when the letter J is pressed.

5. Hold down the SHIFT key and press the P key. Next to the letter is a set of quotation marks in red. When you hold down SHIFT and press the P key, the quotation marks appear on the screen.

6. Type in the name of the program you want to **LOAD**. The name, in our example, is SUM. The name must be typed very precisely. Be careful of spelling or typing mistakes. One error can cause the program not to **LOAD**.

7. Hold down the SHIFT key and press the P key again so that there are quotation marks at the end of the program name. Your screen should look like Figure 4.4.

8. Press the ENTER key on the computer.

9. Set the volume control at a mid-range level and press the PLAY button on the recorder.

Figure 4.4 LOAD command screen display.

The screen will have thin black diagonal lines crossed with wider black lines. If the program loads properly, the TV screen should look like Figure 4.5. The screen will flutter while the program loads, and the design on the screen may change slightly (you may be tempted to reach for the vertical and horizontal controls on the TV, but it really is supposed to roll like that). If the screen does not look like Figure 4.5, then the program probably is not loading. See the section on Trouble Shooting at the end of this chapter for suggestions on what to do if the program doesn't **LOAD**.

Figure 4.5 Screen display during **LOAD**.

Some programs have an auto-run command that lets the program work, or **RUN**, as soon as it is loaded. If that's the case, then the program automatically executes. If your screen is blank except for a message in the lower left hand corner (a 0/0 report code that says the program loaded), then the program does not have an auto-run feature. Your screen may look like Figure 4.6. Press ENTER and the program will be listed at the top of the screen.

If you want to **RUN** the program press the R key to get the key word **RUN** and then press ENTER.

0/0

Figure 4.6 Program message without auto-**RUN**.

TROUBLE SHOOTING

Frequently, the program will not **LOAD**. You must then try to find out why it didn't **LOAD** and how to correct the mistake. Often the only thing to do is stop the recorder, rewind the tape, and begin again. If the computer is still trying to **LOAD** the program, unplug the power, plug it back in, and get your inverse-K cursor at the bottom of the screen. Now try again.

First check for a spelling or typing error in the loading instruction. Are there quotation marks at the beginning and end of the program name? There should not be any spaces between the quotation marks and the program name. Is the program name spelled correctly? The name must be exact.

If you find an error in spelling or typing, start over with the loading steps described earlier.

Another factor that may be causing the mistake is the volume setting on the cassette recorder. The best way to adjust it is to try, try, again. Fortunately, it is usually not necessary to run through an entire program to determine if the volume is correct and the program is loading. If, after about 15 seconds into the program, the TV screen doesn't look like Figure 4.5, then it isn't going to **LOAD**. Adjust the volume setting and start again. It may be necessary to go through this process several times before the right level is located. Once the screen shows the correct pattern, mark the volume control setting (we put fingernail polish on the control knob of our recorder to indicate the exact setting).

Sometimes, rearranging the cords that connect the recorder to the computer will help. It is possible that they are serving as an antenna and picking up interference from the television or the computer. The interference confuses the computer because it can't tell which signals are data and which are interference. Another problem some owners report is electrical "noise" from extra memory modules. Some 16K memory modules (including those from Sinclair and Timex), produce interference when they are attached to the back of the computer. If you are having trouble getting your first program loaded and have an optional memory module plugged in, try loading without the module. **SAVE** a very short program that does not require use of the extra memory and then use the short program to get your volume and tone controls set correctly. When **LOAD** works without the extra memory, plug it back in and see if it will work with the memory connected. A program saved without (or with) extra memory plugged in will not load when extra memory is added (or disconnected). You may have to **SAVE** your short program again so that the **SAVE** and **LOAD** conditions of the program are the same (i.e., both done with extra memory installed or both done without extra memory installed).

Once you get the program to **LOAD**, the most difficult technique for using the TS1000 is mastered. The sequence for loading all programs is the same. Patience is sometimes necessary to find the volume setting, but after that the routine is always the same: press the **LOAD** key, type the name of the program (remember the quotation marks at the beginning and end of the name), press the PLAY button on the recorder, and press the ENTER key on the computer. The next step is to learn how to store, or **SAVE**, programs.

NOTE: The instructions provided in this chapter tell you to type in the name of the program, between quotation marks, after the key word **LOAD**. A simpler approach, however, is simply to use the key word **LOAD** followed by two sets of quotation marks (i.e., **LOAD** "") and press ENTER. The computer will listen to the tones on the tape and load the first program it finds into memory. You may find that you prefer this shorter procedure.

CHAPTER 5

Saving Programs on Cassette

In Chapter 4 you learned how to **LOAD** programs from a cassette into the memory of the TS1000 computer. This chapter teaches you how to store programs for future use.

What exactly does **SAVE** mean? The key word **SAVE** tells the computer to take the program currently in the memory of the computer and record it (as a series of tones) on a cassette. Once a program is properly saved you will be able to reload it into the memory of the computer and use it again by using the key word **LOAD**. If you have written The Great American Computer Program you will not want to type it into the computer each time it is used. Saving a program on cassette gives you a permanent copy of the program that can be directly read by the computer.

Just to get some experience with saving a program, type in the following short example on your TS1000:

10 **PRINT** "THIS IS A TEST"
20 **PRINT** "OF THE SAVE COMMAND"

Make certain the computer and cassette are properly connected (see Chapter 2 and/or Chapter 4). Also make sure the volume control is at the right setting (the setting you use to **LOAD** should also work for **SAVE** – see Chapter 4 to determine this setting). Actually, the setting of the tone and volume controls on most modern cassette recorders has no effect on recording level since automatic circuits adjust the recording level. Some recorders, however, are controlled by the volume control setting. You will need to read the instructions that came with your recorder to determine just what controls your recorder.

SAVING STEPS

Below are the steps to follow to **SAVE** the program:

1. Position the tape at a blank spot on the cassette. Some people store many different programs on the same cassette tape in the belief that they are being thrifty. This is not always as economical as it seems. It is very easy to record a new program over part or all of an old program that you wanted to keep. In addition, there is no convenient way to quickly and accurately find the fifth program on a tape that contains eight programs. You could use the digital counter to mark the beginning of each program and then write the counter number beside the program name on the cassette label. This does work, but it can be tedious (and you can forget to do it).

Our advice is to buy good quality, name brand cassettes, and buy short ones such as C-10, C-20, or C-30. Then record only one program on each side of the tape. That may sound wasteful, but it can save you a great deal of grief and time. If only one program is on each side of a tape you will not run the danger of recording over a program you wanted to keep. And you will not spend time trying to search through a tape to find the correct program on a tape that has many programs recorded on it.

There are only two things to keep in mind. First, be sure to label your cassettes so that you know what is on each one. Many music stores sell inexpensive stick on labels that are cut to fit standard cassettes. Second, many cassettes have a short section of clear "leader" at each end. If the cassettes you use have such a clear leader on them, you will want to use the fast forward control to move past that leader before you record a program. This part of the tape does not record, and your program will not be saved if the beginning is on the leader.

2. With the inverse-K cursor present, press the S key (**SAVE** appears in the lower left hand side of the TV screen).

3. Now, name your program. It is suggested that the name have some relevance to the program so when you want to **LOAD** the file later, you can easily remember what you called the program. Call the example program here TEST.

4. Now type the name of the program and enclose it in quotation marks (e.g., "TEST"). Your screen should now contain SAVE "TEST" at the bottom.

5. Press the RECORD button on your recorder. Some recorders require that RECORD and PLAY be pressed at the same time. Follow the directions for your machine.

6. After about 3 to 5 seconds, press the ENTER key on the computer. At first there will be nothing but gray or black on the TV screen. Don't panic, it's supposed to look like that! After a few seconds the screen should show some thin, fluttery black and white lines. This interference on the television screen is caused by the transmission of data from the computer to the recorder. The process is working!

7. When the program has been saved, the following appears at the bottom of the screen:

0/0

This merely tells you that the computer believes it has done its job. When this message appears, press the STOP button on the recorder.

Now your program is saved. It is always a good idea to make a second copy of your program. You could make another copy of the program on the same tape or on another tape. If you make the second copy on the same tape use the fast forward button to move the tape well beyond the point where the first copy of the program ends (note the location of the second copy by writing the counter number on the cassette label).

Another bit of advice: after you have saved a program twice, try to **LOAD** it (see Chapter 4 for instructions on loading). Never assume that a program has been properly saved if it is important to you. You must check the success of an attempt to **SAVE** a program by using the **LOAD** command. The **LOAD** command destroys whatever program is in memory at the time. That means you will find out that an attempt to **SAVE** a program has gone awry only after you have erased the program from the memory of the computer!

TROUBLE SHOOTING

If the program didn't **SAVE**, a couple of things may have gone wrong. Below is a list of possibilities and ways of correcting mistakes:

- **wrong command**   Make certain that the S key is pressed and that the word **SAVE** appears.

- **no quotation marks**   Are there quotation marks at the beginning and end of the program name?
- **volume or tone control**   Start with the same settings you use for loading programs. If the program still doesn't **SAVE**, you may need to adjust the settings. With most recorders, however, volume and tone settings will not affect saving.
- **bad tape**   It's possible that the cassette is worn or is not of good enough quality to reproduce the computer sounds. Try another tape.
- **cassette recorder problems**   As a tape recorder is used dirt and oxide build up on the playback and recording heads. In addition, the heads can become magnetized and thus record poorly. There are head cleaning kits and head demagnetizers that will help you get your recorder in shape to record programs reliably. Some recorders will not work with the TS1000 if both the MIC and EAR cables are connected. Some users find it necessary to connect the MIC cable only when they **SAVE** a program and the EAR cable only when they **LOAD** a program.

It is also possible that your recorder is not compatible with the TS1000. Some recorders pick up a hum as well as program data when they are used with the TS1000. If that is the case with your recorder, the only option may be to use a different recorder.

Good luck.

CHAPTER 6

Programming in BASIC

This is the first of two chapters that deal specifically with the popular computer language called BASIC. We assume that at this point you have already read Chapter 3 and that you are familiar with the procedures for correcting and editing programs as you type them. A review of the material in Chapter 3 would be helpful before proceeding.

THE PURPOSE OF CHAPTERS 6 AND 7

There are at least two hundred books currently in print that teach you how to write programs in BASIC. There are at least ten books that deal specifically with programming the TS1000 in BASIC. We will not try to teach you how to write BASIC programs on your computer. Instead, the goal of Chapters 6 and 7 is to introduce you to the concept of BASIC and its use on the TS1000. In addition, the chapters provide you with enough knowledge to take BASIC programs written for the TS1000 and use them yourself. There are many books of BASIC programs for the Timex/Sinclair computer available and several magazines (see Chapter 10) that regularly publish programs for the TS1000. After reading the next two chapters, you should be able to understand how BASIC programs work and you should be able to take a TS1000 BASIC program in a book or magazine, type it on your computer and use it. You will know enough BASIC to *debug* a program that isn't working as it should and even make changes or enhancements that interest you.

HOW TO USE THIS CHAPTER

It would be possible for you to plow through these two chapters without a computer and learn some BASIC. Our advice, however, is to read the BASIC chapters in front of the computer. Learn what all the new terms mean, and use your computer to do the examples scattered through the reading. Don't try to memorize definitions and instructions. Practice enough so that working in BASIC is comfortable for you. It is not necessary to be able to say off the top of your head what **GOSUB** 140 means; you only need to know where to look for that information. BASIC will become a familiar second language through experience, not memorization.

This introduction to BASIC is not intended to be a comprehensive tutorial on all aspects of programming in this versatile language. If the material presented here intrigues you there are several good books on the topic of programming the TS1000 in BASIC. dilithium Press, for example, publishes *Using and Programming Your Timex Sinclair Computer* by Ken Knecht.

INTRODUCTION TO BASIC

There are several important differences between the language spoken by a computer and regular English. In English the meaning will usually be clear even if a word or two were misspelled. BASIC and other computer languages are not so forgiving. You must say precisely what you intend to, and say it exactly as the computer expects.

Another difference is in the way punctuation is handled. Commas, semicolons, and periods clarify the meaning of written English, but the rules for their use vary. You would be able to understand a letter from Uncle Harry even if he managed to write a whole page without a comma or period. In BASIC these punctuation marks are often as important as the letters and numbers. Leaving out one comma can prevent an entire program from running properly.

Finally, English is a very rich language. There are usually several words that have similar meanings; a 1956 Chevrolet could appropriately be called a car, auto, automobile, or vehicle. BASIC is not so well endowed. Often there is only one way of saying something.

The words BASIC understands are called "key words." To make the computer do something, these key words are used to make up statements. Statements correspond to sentences in English. The term *statement* actually has two uses in computer programming. It can mean the same thing as program line, and it is often used in much the same way key word is used here. Three examples of statements (i.e., program lines) are given below:

    10 **LET** A = 2
    20 **LET** B = 4
    30 **PRINT** A + B
    RUN

Each statement is preceded by a line number. When a computer is told to **RUN** a program it begins with the statement that has the lowest line number and follows the instructions given in that statement. It then proceeds through the program until all the statements have been executed. When it reaches line 30 in our example it will do the arithmetic requested (2 + 4) and print the results. Type in this program on your TS1000. If some of the details of typing in programs are fuzzy you may want to review Chapter 3.

The three statements you typed in make up a simple program. A program is a set of instructions or statements that tell the computer how to solve a particular problem. When the three-statement program is typed in, press the R key to get the key word **RUN** at the bottom of the screen. Then press the ENTER key. If the computer responds by printing 6, you are off and running.

At this point we have several new terms. BASIC is a popular computer language. It enables the computer to understand a number of special or key words such as **LET** and **RUN**. BASIC also has a set of rules about how punctuation marks are used. Using these rules and the key words BASIC understands, a person can write programs that the computer can execute or carry out. Programs are made up of lines or statements, each of which begins with a number (the line number). Statements contain key words, used according to the rules of BASIC.

You tell a computer you want it to execute a program (follow the instructions in the program) by giving it the key word **RUN**. This is the normal way a computer is used. There is, however, another way. If you simply type in the following line:

PRINT 2 + 2

the computer will print the results of adding 2 and 2 immediately after you press the ENTER key. If you do not put a line number in front of a statement, the computer assumes you want the instructions carried out immediately. This method of using a computer is sometimes called the *calculator mode* or the *immediate mode*. It is handy since it lets you use the computer as you would a pocket calculator. The key word **PRINT**, if it is used to tell the computer to do something immediately, is called a *command*. If **PRINT** is part of a program it is called a *statement* in most textbooks. Most of the key words in BASIC can function as either commands or statements. A few, such as **FOR, NEXT, PAUSE,** and **SCROLL** can only be used effectively in programs (i.e., as statements). The key word **CONT**, on the other hand, can only be used as a command.

In the next section you will learn more about some of the most frequently used key words in the TS1000 version of BASIC.

PROGRAM CONTROL COMMANDS

Several of the key words available in BASIC are used to tell the computer how to manage its work. They are listed below with a description of the job they do:

ENTER. This command has its own key on the keyboard. **ENTER** is used to tell the computer you have finished typing in a line of instructions at the bottom of the screen. When you press the **ENTER** key the computer looks at the line. If it finds an error, it places an inverse-S cursor at the point where the error occurs and waits for you to correct it and press **ENTER** again. If no error is found the computer checks for a line number. If there is one, the program line is placed at the top of the screen. If there is no line number the computer attempts to execute the instructions immediately.

RUN. This command has already been used several times. When you give the **RUN** command, it tells the computer you want it to execute the instructions contained in the program currently in the computer's memory. Normally, **RUN** tells the computer to begin with the instructions in the line with the lowest number. There is a variation of **RUN**, however, that specifies which line number to begin with. If you tell the computer **RUN** 70, the computer will start executing instructions in lines 70 and above. Any instructions with line numbers less than 70 would not be executed.

NEW. There are times when you want to stop what you are doing and start over. One way to accomplish that is to pull the plug on the computer. Another way is to use the command **NEW**. **NEW** erases any program currently in the computer's memory. You can then start fresh with nothing left of the old program. Before you use **NEW** be sure you really do want to erase everything in memory. Once it is done, it's done.

CLEAR. This key word lets you erase values assigned to variables without erasing the program in memory. For example, if you have an instruction such as **LET** A = 5, A will equal 5 after you **RUN** the program once. If you **RUN** the program again, A will already equal 5 when the program starts. If you want to clear the memory of all variables (such as A) and their values (such as 5), use **CLEAR**. You can use **CLEAR** as a command or as a statement.

CLS. This key word leaves the program intact and has no effect on variables or their values. It does, however, clear the screen. It can be used as a command or statement.

SAVE and **LOAD**. These key words are used to **LOAD** and **SAVE** material from cassettes. They are dealt with in detail in Chapters 4 and 5.

LIST. This command tells the computer that you wish to see the lines of the current program displayed on the video display. You get a "listing" of the program. **LIST** will cause the entire program to be listed, if it contains less than 24 lines. If your program is more than 24 lines long the computer can't get all of it onto the screen at once. **LIST** will show you 24 lines. Which 24 lines it shows will depend on where the "program cursor" is located. The program cursor is the dark square with a > sign in it. You will find it just after the line number on one of the program lines at the top of the screen. You can use the up and down arrow keys to move the program cursor to another line. The line that contains the program cursor is always displayed by **LIST**. If it is at the bottom of the program the top lines will not appear; if it is at the top the lines at the end of the program won't be visible. If you use **LIST** and a 5/0 report code appears in the bottom left corner of the screen, that means that there is more program that can't be displayed. If you want to see a particular section of the program listing you can use the **LIST #**

format. The # symbol stands for a line number. If, for example, you type **LIST** 16 (and press ENTER), the computer will begin its listing at line 16 and display as many of the lines below 16 as it can. You may have to practice a bit to get used to how **LIST** works with long programs.

LLIST. This command works much like **LIST**, but it sends the listing of the program to a printer instead of the video display.

EDIT. This is a very useful key word. It lets you take a line out of a program and bring it to the bottom of the screen for editing. To see how it works type in two or three program lines with the line numbers 10, 20, and 30. Is the program cursor in line 30? Move it to Line 20. Now hold down the shift key and press the **EDIT** key (1 in the top left). That should bring line 20 to the bottom of the screen. Now you can use any of the editing features discussed in Chapter 3 to modify the line. When you finish editing press ENTER and the line will be placed in the program, complete with your corrections.

If you move the program cursor to line 10 and press **EDIT**, you can modify or correct that line too. You can also change the line number of statement 10. Bring line 10 to the bottom of the screen by using **EDIT**. Move the cursor over to the far left of line 10 and press 8. That makes the line number 810. Now press ENTER. The computer keeps line 10 in the program as it was, but it adds a new line (line 810) to the end of the program. This is a handy trick if you need to type in many lines that are very similar. You can type in one line and then create the others with **EDIT**. This feature of **EDIT** is also handy when you intend to type in line 120, but type in 20 instead. Use **EDIT** to get 20 down to the bottom, add 1 to make it 120 and press ENTER. Then type in 20 and press ENTER to get rid of your bogus line 20. If you "wiped out" the real line 20 you will have to type it in again.

PAUSE. There are times when you want the computer to wait a bit before proceeding. **PAUSE** tells the computer to do just that. It must be followed by a number (e.g., **PAUSE** 30). In the United States the number after **PAUSE** tells the computer how many 1/60's of a second to pause. Thus **PAUSE** 600 would tell the computer to wait 10 seconds before proceeding. Actually, the timing is not that accurate. The computer will pause for slightly over 9 seconds. **PAUSE** uses the number of times the computer refreshes the television display as a reference mark for its time. In the United States this occurs about 60 times a second. If your version of the TS1000 uses a PAL or SECAM television, the timing on **PAUSE** will be different.

CONT. This is short for continue. If a program takes up more than 22 lines of display while running, the computer will stop executing the program after the 22nd line. You must use the key word **CONT** to get it to continue processing. Type in this program to see how **CONT** works (type **NEW** to clear out any programs currently in memory):

```
10 FOR X = 1 TO 50
20 PRINT "ANOTHER LINE ";X
30 NEXT X
```

RUN the program. It will put 22 lines on the screen and stop with a 5/20 report. That means it has run out of display space on the screen (5) and has stopped at line 20. Press **CONT**, then press ENTER and the computer will continue executing the program. This time it will get to ANOTHER LINE 44 and stop again. Press **CONT** ENTER and it will continue to 50 and stop with a 0/30 report which means that no problems occurred (0) and line 30 was the last one used. Press ENTER now and the program will be listed at the top of the screen. This program is used to illustrate how the key words **FAST** and **SLOW** operate as well.

SCROLL. Another way of dealing with the problem posed by a program that uses all 22 lines on the screen is the key word **SCROLL**. When you use the key word **SCROLL**, the computer pushes one line at a time off the top of the screen. This makes room for one more line at the bottom of the screen.

FAST and **SLOW.** The demonstration program described under the explanation of **CONT** runs fairly slowly. Type the program in again if you don't have it in the computer and RUN it once more. Note how much time it takes. Now use the key word **FAST** (SHIFT F, ENTER). RUN the program now. Two things should be different. First, the screen will go blank when you tell the computer to RUN the program. Second, the first 22 lines of output will appear all at once, and it will take less time than it did before. Press **CONT** and ENTER to see the next set of lines. Press **CONT** and ENTER once more and the program finishes its work.

The TS1000 doesn't have much circuitry and the chips that are used to process the program also serve the video display. In the standard or **SLOW** mode the processing of a program will only take place when the computer can take a quick (microsecond) break from supporting the television display. The **SLOW** mode is just that, slow. If you tell the computer you want to use the **FAST** mode, the computer devotes all its time to processing program instructions when necessary. This inattention to the video display is the reason for the blank screen when it is processing.

Now press ENTER to call the listing of the program back to the screen and type in this line:

    40 **REM** END OF PROGRAM

Each time you press a key the screen flickers. The computer must momentarily let display support fall by the wayside while it deals with your input. The flicker is distracting to most people so program writing is generally done in the slow mode. If you use the **SLOW** key word now (SHIFT D ENTER) the computer will return to the slower mode of operation.

Both **SLOW** and **FAST** can be used as commands or as statements. You may want to use the **FAST** key word in a program just before complicated processing instructions are executed. Then use the **SLOW** key word at the end of that section of the program. Since **FAST** causes the screen to go blank, it cannot be used for graphics displays that simulate movement. **FAST**, however, is preferred when you place a heavy processing demand on the computer.

BREAK. The command **BREAK** is used to stop a program during execution. If you tell the computer to RUN a program and then decide, while the computer is carrying out your instructions, that you want it to stop the program before it has finished, just press the **BREAK** key. Execution will stop and the report code will be D/#. The D indicates the program stopped because **BREAK** was pressed and # indicates the line number where execution was terminated. **BREAK** is used only as a command. See the discussion of **INPUT** later in this chapter for instructions on how to stop a program that is trying to execute an **INPUT** instruction.

STOP. This key word is a statement that works a lot like the command **BREAK**. A program line like 45 **STOP** will cause program execution to stop at line 45. If you want the computer to continue executing the program after it gets to the line containing the **STOP** instruction, just use the **CONT** key word. The computer will pick up where it left off and continue execution.

CLERICAL INSTRUCTIONS
PRINT, LPRINT, PRINT AT, COPY, TAB,
Comma, Semicolon

Now that you've gotten the hang of it we'll pick up the pace a bit. In the following sections additional key words and programming rules will be presented and explained. Generally the explanation will be associated with a short demonstration program like the one used to show you how **CONT** works. If this is your first venture into programming we advise you to read the explanations carefully and RUN each of the example programs.

PRINT. This statement causes the computer to print out or display whatever follows **PRINT**. You have used it several times already. If material following **PRINT** is enclosed in quotation marks, the computer will print it exactly as typed. The material inside the quotation marks is called a string or a literal string. The instruction **PRINT** "THIS IS A TEST" would cause the computer to print the string THIS IS A TEST on the screen.

If there are no quotation marks around the material to be printed, the computer behaves a little differently. Consider the problem below:

```
10 LET THIS = 30
20 PRINT THIS
```

Type in the program and RUN it. Line 10 tells the computer that you want to use a variable named THIS and that you want to make THIS equal to 30. Line 20 does not print the name of the variable (THIS). Instead, it prints the value of THIS which is 30. Whether you use quotation marks or not will make a big difference in what the computer does.

Commas and Semicolons

Add the following lines to the two lines you typed in to see how **PRINT** works:

```
30 PRINT "THIS EQUALS";THIS
40 PRINT "THIS EQUALS  ";THIS
50 PRINT "THIS EQUALS  ",THIS
60 PRINT "THIS EQUALS",THIS
```

Note that the only difference between line 30 and line 40 is the space between the S in EQUALS and the semicolon. Now RUN the program. Your display should look like this:

```
30
THIS EQUALS30
THIS EQUALS 30
THIS EQUALS          30
THIS EQUALS          30
```

0/50

The 30 on the first line of the display came from line 20. Lines 30 and 40 produce almost identical displays. The literal string THIS EQUALS was printed first by both lines. Then the value of the variable THIS was printed. In line 30 a space inside the quotation marks makes the line neater and easier to read because the number 30 is not directly up against the S in EQUALS. The semicolon that follows the literal string tells the computer to print whatever comes next immediately after the last item printed. If you use a semicolon to separate two items that are to be printed, you must add any spaces needed yourself (i.e., inside the quotation marks of the literal string).

Lines 50 and 60 produce exactly the same results even though one has a space inside the quotation marks and one does not. Why? The key lies in using the comma rather than the semicolon as a separator. The TS1000 divides the screen into two "areas" or zones. The first zone begins on the far left of the display. The second zone begins at the 16th position on the screen. A comma instructs the computer to begin printing whatever follows in the next print zone rather than right up against the material already printed. Thus, a comma generally separates material while a semicolon puts it together.

Both commas and semicolons show no respect for the end of a line. If you tell the computer to print too much material to fit on a line, the computer will type all that it can on one line and put the rest on the next line. The program below illustrates the point. Use the key word **NEW** and then type it in:

```
 5 FOR X = 1 TO 30
10 PRINT "AND";
20 PRINT "YET";
30 PRINT "ANOTHER";
40 NEXT X
```

RUN the program and you will see that it fills up 12 lines on the display and spills over a bit to the 13th line. The three literal strings AND, YET, and ANOTHER are printed end to end until the program loop has been executed 30 times. Now add the following lines:

```
 50 PRINT
 60 PRINT
 70 FOR B = 1 TO 8
 80 PRINT "EVEN",
 90 PRINT "MORE",
100 NEXT B
```

RUN the expanded program. The same letters as before appear at the top of the screen. Then lines 50 and 60 give us a blank line (50 gets us off the line with ANOTHER on it, 60 skips one line). Then the second **FOR NEXT** loop prints a pattern of EVEN   MORE on the screen eight times. The comma on lines 80 and 90 causes the computer to space over and print material at the beginning of each of the two print zones.

You may want to experiment with the **PRINT** instruction and with commas and semicolons to get familiar with how they work.

A final note on **PRINT**. If you tell the computer to print something and don't put a comma or semicolon after it (e.g., **PRINT** "HELLO") the computer will automatically go to the beginning of the next line when it encounters the next **PRINT** instruction.

LPRINT and **COPY**. The key word **LPRINT** works in the same way **PRINT** does, except that it sends material to a printer instead of to the video display. **COPY** also sends material to the printer. When you tell the computer to **COPY** it sends an exact copy of the video display to the printer. This is called a *screen dump* on some computers.

PRINT AT. This is a variation of our old favorite, **PRINT**. The screen display on the TS1000 is divided into 22 lines of 32 characters each. If you wish, you can tell the computer exactly where you want something printed by using **PRINT AT** instead of **PRINT**. The standard format for **PRINT AT** is:

PRINT AT #,#; material to be printed

The first # indicates the line number (0 to 21 with 0 at the top of the screen); the second # specifies the character position on the line (0 to 31 with 0 on the far left). You get **PRINT AT** by using the **PRINT** key word on the P key. Then hold down the SHIFT key and press the FUNCTION key. The cursor will change to an inverse-F, and you can then press the C key to get AT. AT is classed as a *function* and appears below the C key. We will discuss functions later. Here is a demonstration program:

10 **PRINT AT** 0,0;"NORTHWEST"
20 **PRINT AT** 21,0;"SOUTHWEST"
30 **PRINT AT** 0,19;"NORTHEAST"
40 **PRINT AT** 21,19;"SOUTHEAST"
50 **PRINT AT** 11,5;"WHICH WAY DID THEY GO?"

When you RUN this program it should put the directions in the four corners of the display and the phrase WHICH WAY DID THEY GO? in the middle of the screen. The **PRINT AT** instruction is a handy way of controlling where the computer prints material. **PRINT AT** does not check to see if something is already printed in the location it is using. It will print over anything already displayed there. In addition, if you tell it to print spaces (e.g., **PRINT** "   ") it will erase anything in the area used by **PRINT AT**.

    TAB. This function is similar to AT. You use it with **PRINT** to control where material is printed on the line. The general format for its use is:

PRINT TAB #; material to be printed

The number following TAB indicates where on the line printing will begin. That number can be anything from 0 (far left side) to 31. **PRINT TAB** 18; "THIS WAY OUT" will cause the literal string to be printed on the left side of the screen. You get **PRINT TAB** by pressing P for the **PRINT** key word and then holding down the SHIFT key and pressing ENTER. This brings up the function cursor (inverse-F) and then you can press P to get TAB. The statement **PRINT TAB** 3;"PING";TAB 22;"PONG" will put PING on one side of the screen and PONG on the other.

GETTING INFORMATION INTO THE COMPUTER

There are three major ways TS1000 BASIC allows you to assign *values* to *variables*. You can do this with the **LET** and **INPUT** statements and with the **INKEY$** function. **LET.** You have already used **LET** several times in the example programs. The general format for **LET** is:

LET variable name = value

The **LET** key word tells the computer what value to associate with a particular variable name. For example, **LET** B = 22 tells the computer that until further notice the variable named B will equal (have the value of) 22.

There are two basic types of variables, numeric and string. In the example above, B is a numeric variable. **LET** B$ = "HELLO" tells the computer that the string variable B$ is to equal HELLO. The $ after B designates the variable as a string variable. If the variable name does not end with a $ the computer assumes it is dealing with a numeric rather than a string variable. The TS1000 will not accept **LET** A = "HELLO" because there is a mismatch between the type of variable specified (numeric or string) and the type of value assigned.

If you assign a value to B (or B$) early in a program (e.g., 10 **LET** B = 22) and then assign another value to B (or B$) later (e.g., 30 **LET** B = 66) the value of B will be the last one assigned (66 in this example).

Up to this point the value assigned with the **LET** statement has been a simple numeric value (22) or a literal string value ("HELLO"). **LET** is actually much more versatile. **LET** can use another variable to assign the value to a new variable (**LET** B = A or **LET** B$ = A$) and it can use an *expression* (**LET** B = 2 + 5). These **LET** instructions are also acceptable:

LET B = B + 2
LET B = B + A

The only restriction in the examples above is the requirement that any variable name on the right side of the equal sign must have been defined previously in the program. The program line 30 **LET** B = B + A is fine if an earlier line defined the value of A (e.g., 10 **LET** A = 95).

Finally, the computer can use variable names that are more complex than A or B$. Both numeric and string variable names must begin with a letter. String variables must end with a $. More complex variable names are often more useful since they can give you an indication of the role of the variable in the program. Here are some examples:

INTEREST   TEST2   NAME$ FSTGAME   BALANCE

Remember that each letter and number in the name of a variable takes up memory space. If you are likely to need most of your memory for a long program, it may be necessary to keep variable names short.

INPUT. When the computer comes to an **INPUT** statement, it stops and waits for the operator to provide it with some data. If **INPUT** is followed by a numeric variable name (e.g., **INPUT** B or **INPUT** BALANCE) the computer expects you to type in a numeric value and press ENTER. If **INPUT** is followed by a string variable name (e.g., **INPUT** B$ or **INPUT** NAME$) the computer expects you to type in a string (don't enclose it in quotation marks) and press ENTER. If you give a string value when the computer expects a numeric value, the computer will reject your input. Here is a short example program:

```
10 PRINT "TYPE IN A NUMBER"
20 INPUT A
30 PRINT A
40 PRINT "TYPE IN A STRING"
50 INPUT A$
60 PRINT A$
```

RUN this program. The screen will display TYPE IN A NUMBER at the top and an inverse-L cursor will appear in the bottom left corner. The computer is waiting for you to type in a numeric variable. If you type in a number and press ENTER the computer will make A equal to the number you typed in. Then it will print that value (line 30). Line 40 tells you to TYPE IN A STRING; line 50 tells the computer to look for a string. Type in TESTING and press ENTER. Note that the inverse-L cursor at the bottom is enclosed in quotation marks. As you type in TESTING it is surrounded by quotation marks which eliminate the need for you to type them. They also tell you that the computer expects a string variable to be input. The computer will print TESTING and end its work with a 0/60 report that indicates it has followed the instructions through line 60 without encountering any errors.

What happens if your input is not what the computer was expecting? RUN the program again and type in TESTING when the computer expects a numeric value. When you press EN-TER the computer gives a 2/10 report at the bottom of the screen. That means there was a problem in line 10. The 2 error code indicates a problem with a variable. In this instance the problem is a mismatch between the variable name (A) and the type of data input (TESTING). Press the ENTER key and the program will be listed at the top of the screen. Now RUN the program again. This time type in 3T4 and press ENTER. Something different happened this time. Instead of stopping, the computer simply refused to accept your input. It put an in-verse-S cursor to the right of the T. Use the right arrow key to move the cursor to the left of the T. Then press the DELETE key and get rid of the T. Now press ENTER. The computer accepts the 34 as a numeric value, prints it on the screen and goes on to lines 40 and 50. Now it is looking for a string variable. Type in 34 and press ENTER. Surprised by the re-sults? The computer accepted 34 as a string with no problems and printed out 34. That means A equals 34 and so does A$. There is a difference in the two variables, however. Add the following two lines to the program:

70 **PRINT** A + 12
80 **PRINT** A$ + 12

When you try to ENTER line 80 the computer rejects it and indicates that there is a syntax error at the end of the line. You cannot add a string variable to a numeric variable. Thus, even though A$ equals 34 you will not be permitted to use it as a numeric variable. To the computer the 34 value of A$ is simply a two character string, not a number. Use the DELETE key to get rid of line 80 — it will not work. Now RUN the program again and use 34 as the value for both A and A$. When the computer gets to line 70 it will print 46 on the screen (34 + 12). The 34 value of A is different from the 34 value of A$. The variable A can be manipulated mathematically while the vari-able A$ cannot.

There is one final point about **INPUT** statements. The key word **BREAK** has been mentioned already as a means of telling the computer to stop executing a program. RUN your program one more time. When the computer asks you to input a value for A, press the **BREAK** key. You get a space instead of a **BREAK** since the cursor at the bottom is an inverse-L instead of an inverse-K. Use the key word **STOP** instead (SHIFT A). The computer will stop executing the program and put the report D/20 at the bottom of the screen. The D error code is used when you interrupt normal execution of the program with a **BREAK** or if you input STOP. If you wish to continue executing the program at this point use the **CONT** key word. (If you want to stop completely press the ENTER key and the program will be listed at the top of the screen.) Press **CONT** and ENTER and the computer will pick up at line 20 again. Type in 34 and press ENTER. Now the computer is looking for a string input. Press the **BREAK** key again. All you get is a space. Now press **STOP** (SHIFT A). **STOP** appears within the quotation marks. Press ENTER. The computer has assigned A$ the value " STOP" instead of stopping the program execution. RUN the program again and give A the value of 34. When the computer asks for string input use the left arrow key to move the inverse-L cursor to the left of the quotation marks. (Make sure you are to the left of the marks rather than to the right.) Now type SHIFT A to get the STOP key word and press EN-TER. The computer stops executing the program and gives a D/40 report. If you press ENTER the program will be displayed at the top of the screen. If you press **CONT** the program will pick up where it left off on line 40 and expect you to type in a string. Getting the computer to stop execution when it is waiting for a string input requires you to move the cursor to the left of the quotation marks. If you type a key word inside quotation marks the computer will simply use the key word as part of the string.

A NOTE ON QUOTATION MARKS IN STRINGS

Suppose you want to use a string that contains a quotation mark. That is a problem since the computer uses the quotation mark to designate the beginning and end of a string. Here is an example:

    20 **LET** B$ = "SO I SAID "NO""

The computer will think that the string value for B$ ends after SAID because there is a quotation mark at that point. There is a way to get around this problem. Normally, you use the quotation marks on the P key. There are also double quotation marks in red on the Q key. If you retype the line above and use the quotes on the Q key (instead of the quotation marks on the P key) just before N and after O, the string will appear as, SO I SAID "NO". The double marks, when embedded in a string (e.g., before NO) show up as simply a quotation mark. If double marks are used at the beginning or end of a string (e.g., after O) they designate the beginning or end of a string and specify that a quotation mark should be added to the string at that point.

INKEY$ AND **GOTO.** One of the problems of using **INPUT** is that you must press ENTER after you have typed in the necessary data. That is usually no great burden, but there are times when pressing ENTER creates problems. Many games, for example, begin with instructions. You tell the computer whether you want instructions or not by pressing one of two keys. Then you tell the computer you have finished reading the instructions by pressing another key. Novices often forget to press the ENTER key in such situations and end up wondering why the program doesn't work. This sort of frustration can be avoided if you use **INKEY$** instead of **INPUT.** Type **NEW** to get rid of any program in the memory of the computer and then type in the program below. It will illustrate the use of **INKEY$**:

```
10 PRINT "NEED INSTRUCTIONS?"
20 PRINT "PRESS Y FOR YES N FOR NO"
30 IF INKEY$ = "Y" THEN GOTO 60
40 IF INKEY$ = "N" THEN GOTO 100
50 GOTO 30
60 PRINT "INSTRUCTIONS PROVIDED HERE"
70 PRINT "PRESS G TO BEGIN GAME"
80 IF INKEY$ = "" THEN GOTO 80
100 PRINT "THE GAME BEGINS HERE"
```

The **INKEY$** function lets you define the value of the string **INKEY$** simply by pressing a key on the keyboard. Line 10 in the example program asks if you need instructions. Line 20 tells you to press the Y key for instructions, and the N key if you don't want them (if you've played the game before and are ready to begin). Lines 20 and 30 check to see if the string **INKEY$** equals Y or N. If it equals Y, the computer follows the **GOTO** instruction and goes to line 60 (where the instructions would be printed). If **INKEY$** equals N, the **GOTO** instruction in line 30 tells the computer to jump to line 100 and begin executing the instructions there. As soon as you press Y or N, the computer follows one of the **GOTO** instructions in lines 20 and 30. The computer will execute lines 20 and 30 before you press Y or N, however. When it does, **INKEY$** will equal nothing since you have not pressed a key. Line 50 sends the computer back to line 30. The program will thus loop through lines 30 through 50 until a key is pressed.

If you press the Y key the computer prints the material in lines 60 and 70. That would usually be a screen of instructions. You are also told to press G when you finish reading the instructions and are ready to play the game. Then we come to line 80:

80 **IF INKEY$** = "" **THEN GOTO** 80

As long as you do not press a key on the keyboard the string variable **INKEY$** will equal nothing. Nothing is indicated by "" which is also called a *null string* since there is nothing between the quotation marks. Thus, unless you press a key the computer will execute the instructions in line 80 over and over. When you do press a key, the **GOTO** 80 instruction in line 80 will not be executed since **INKEY$** does not equal "". The computer goes on to the next line of instructions which is line 100. Although the computer tells the person to use the G key, any key will cause the computer to move on. This was done for several reasons. You don't want to tell the user to press any key because **INKEY$** treats the space key as **BREAK** and stops execution. Even if the user happens to miss the G key and presses another key we can still be fairly sure that he or she is ready to begin the game.

INKEY$** does have its limitations. It can only have a one character value (**INKEY$ can equal A, B, or 1, and so on, but it cannot equal AVERAGE). In addition, the computer quickly scans the keyboard to see what key is pressed when it encounters **INKEY$**. That means you must write the program in such a way that the computer will check the keyboard over and over until a key is pressed. Consider the example below:

10 **PRINT INKEY$**
20 **GOTO** 10

If you RUN this program you will probably get a series of question marks down the left side of the screen and a 5/10 report. The question marks are there because you were pressing the ENTER key and the ? is the value given to **INKEY$** when the ENTER key is pressed. If you were relatively slow about lifting your finger off the ENTER key there may be as many as 22 question marks on the screen. Faster fingers may produce only four or five question marks. However, when you remove your finger from ENTER the program keeps reading the **INKEY$** input and puts blank spaces on each line instead of question marks since no key was being pressed. Add line 5 to the program and change line 20:

    5 IF INKEY$ = "" THEN GOTO 10
    20 GOTO 5

Now if you RUN the program you will still get a few question marks (from the ENTER key) but you will also be able to press other keys on the keyboard and see what they produce. There is still a problem, however. If you press the C key you probably get several C's on the screen because the **INKEY$** instruction is executed several times before you can get your finger off C. Although it is possible to get around this problem (for instance, by adding 18 **PAUSE** 10 to the program) it is a serious limitation of **INKEY$**.

MATH EXPRESSIONS AND ORDER OF CALCULATION

BASIC uses the normal symbols to indicate addition (+) and subtraction (−). Multiplication is indicated by an asterisk (*) and division by a slash (/). The expression:

    LET A = 5*4 + 1

means A equals five times four plus one. The expression:

    LET B = 20/4 − 1

means B equals twenty divided by four minus one. The variable A thus equals 21 and B equals 4. There is one more math symbol that is frequently seen in programs. Look at the two examples below:

    LET R = 5*5*5   LET R = 5**3

Both these expressions equal 125. The first uses a series of multiplication symbols to obtain the answer. The second expression is read as five raised to the third power or five cubed.

The symbol for powers is two asterisks (**). Note that the asterisk (*) is on the B key while the double asterisk (**) is on the H key. You cannot create a double asterisk to indicate a power computation by striking the * on the B key twice.

When BASIC is used to do a series of math operations it follows a standard sequence in doing them. All the power computations are done first, then the multiplication and division is finished. Finally, the addition and subtraction is computed. A handy mnemonic to remember the standard sequence is Please My Dear Aunt Sally for Power, Multiply, Divide, Add, and Subtract. When there are several of the same types of math to be done, the computer will do the work on the left first and then work across to the right.

Sometimes the standard order of computing is not the order needed to solve the problem correctly. It can be changed by the use of parentheses. The computer will do all the computations inside the parentheses (regardless of the type) before doing the work outside the parentheses. Consider the two expressions below:

PRINT 6*4−3   **PRINT** 6*(4−3)

The first expression produces 21 because the multiplication is done first, then the three is subtracted from the result. The second expression produces 6 because the subtraction is done first (4−3), then the multiplication 6*1. If an expression has several sets of parentheses the computer will do everything inside the innermost set of parentheses first, then work in the next and so on, and finally do the work outside any parentheses. When using parentheses be sure there is one right parenthesis for every left parenthesis, otherwise the computer will report an error.

TYPES OF NUMBERS

The BASIC used in the TS1000 can deal with several types of numbers. Here are examples of the types of numbers it accepts:

5	positive integer or "whole" number
−5	negative integer or "whole" number
345.55	positive decimal number
−345.55	negative decimal number
4.33E+5	positive number in scientific notation
4.33E−5	negative number in scientific notation

The last two numbers may require some explaining. Scientific notation is a means of writing very large and very small numbers in a way that conserves space. The number 4.55E + 5 is the same as 455000. You make the conversion by moving the decimal five places to the right. The number 4.33E − 5 is the same as .0000433 because you move the decimal point five places to the left. If the TS1000 encounters a number so large that it cannot display it in normal fashion, it will convert it to scientific notation. In your programming you can also use scientific notation when it is convenient.

A NOTE ON REPORT CODES

Report Codes have been mentioned several times in this chapter. A standard Report Code is 0 followed by a slash and another number appearing in the bottom left of the screen. The Report Code 0/120 tells you that the computer has completed execution of a program (that is when Report Codes are normally given), and that the last program line used was 120.

If the computer runs into difficulty it may stop execution of a program prematurely and give you a Report Code other than 0. The code 5/100, for example, means that the computer stopped while it was working on line 100. The reason it stopped was that the screen was filled (report 5). Appendix A contains an explanation of what the Report Codes mean and some suggestions for how to correct the problems.

CHAPTER 7

More BASIC

MAKING DECISIONS AND COMPARISONS

BASIC has several ways of comparing one variable to another and making decisions. The most important of these are **IF THEN, GOSUB,** and **FOR NEXT.**

IF THEN

Remember the explanation of the key word **INKEY$** in the preceding chapter? The example program used several **IF THEN** statements to make decisions about what to do next. The key words **IF** and **THEN** are used together to enable the computer to make many different types of decisions.

IF THEN is more like a family of instructions than just one statement. Here is a typical example of an **IF THEN** statement:

50 **IF** X < N **THEN PRINT** X$,X

Line 50 above looks at the value of X. **IF** X is less than (<) N, **THEN** the computer will **PRINT** the string X$ and the value of the numeric variable X. The **IF** in line 50 is used to specify a condition. If that condition exists the action specified in the **THEN** part is performed. There are several types of **IF THEN** statements.

The **IF THEN** statement can involve any combination of the conditions and actions listed, and it can make comparisons that involve values (**IF** S = 5), variables (**IF** X = G), strings (**IF** P$ = "YES"), or expressions (**IF** X/B = Z/A). When the condition exists the computer will proceed across the line and take whatever action is specified. If the condition does not exist the computer moves on to the next line in the program without taking the action called for in the **IF THEN** statement. **IF THEN** allows a programmer to perform "conditional branching." That is, the computer will do something if and only if certain conditions exist.

IF	**THEN**
The Condition	The Action
< less than	**GOTO**
> greater than	**PRINT**
= equals	**LET**
< = less than or equal	**INPUT**
> = greater than or equal	**GOSUB**
< > not equal	**RETURN**
NOT	**STOP**
AND	**CLS**
OR	**PAUSE**
	PLOT
	UNPLOT

Here are some examples of typical **IF THEN** statements that use various combinations of "conditions" and "actions."

IF B > A **THEN PRINT** A – If B is greater than A then the value of A will appear on the video screen.

IF A$ < > B$ **THEN LET** A$ = "" – If the literal string A$ is not equal to the literal string B$ then A$ will equal a null string.

IF (5*45/K) < = B/K **THEN INPUT** A – If 5 times 45 divided by K is less than or equal to B divided by K then the value of A will be input.

Comparisons Involving Strings

Several of the examples above compare strings (e.g., A$ = "YES" or A$ < > B$). Comparisons involving the equal sign (=) and the not-equal sign (< >) are relatively easy to understand. The two strings must be exactly the same to meet the equal condition, and a single difference (e.g., CAN NOT versus CANNOT) will cause the not-equal-to condition to be met. What about comparisons involving the greater-than or less-than symbols? What does

IF A$ < B$ **THEN GOTO** 120

mean? Suppose A$ equals THESE and B$ equals THIS? Would the action after THEN be executed? Logically, you might assume that since there are five letters in A$ and only four in B$ then the condition would not be met since A$ is not "less than" B$. That, however, is not how the comparison works. When a greater-than or less-than comparison is to be made the computer does it alphabetically. The letter A is "less than" the letter B because A comes first in the alphabet. Thus when the comparison of A$ and B$ is made the computer will find the first two letters of the string to be equal, but the third letter in A$ is E while it is I in B$. E comes before I in the alphabet and that makes A$ less than B$.

The Use of Logical Operators

All of the examples cited above used standard arithmetic operators such as "equal to" and "greater than." Most readers are probably familiar with arithmetic operators. There are three *conditional* operators, however, that may not be familiar. They are **NOT**, **AND**, and **OR**. These are logical operators which come from a branch of mathematics called Boolean algebra (named after the mathematician Boole who developed the concepts). Here are some examples using **AND** and **OR**:

IF A$ = "YES" AND A < 34 THEN GOTO 135 – If the string A$ equals YES and, in addition, A is less than 34, then the computer will **GOTO** line 135 and begin executing the instructions found there.

The **AND** operator allows you to set up two conditions for execution of the instructions after **THEN**. If you use **AND** it tells the computer that both conditions must be met before the instructions after **THEN** are executed.

It is also perfectly acceptable to set up more than two conditions using **AND**. Here is an example:

IF A = 1 AND B = 2 AND C = 3 THEN PRINT "EVERYTHING CHECKS OUT" – If A equals 1, B equals 2, and C equals 3, the string will be printed.

In this example all three conditions must be met. If one of the variables has a value other than the one specified after the equals sign, the action after **THEN** will not be taken.

Now let's look at **OR**. Here is an example:

IF A\$ = "YES" **OR** A < 35 **THEN GOTO** 135 – If the string A\$ equals YES or if A < 35 then the computer will **GOTO** line 135 and begin executing the instructions stored there.

The **OR** operator tells the computer to execute the instructions after **THEN** if either of the conditions are met. Thus if A\$ equals YES and A equals 121, the action will be carried out. If A\$ equals NO and A equals 34, the action will be carried out. If A\$ equals YES and A equals 34, the action will also be carried out, since the condition specified by **OR** is more than fulfilled. The only way the action after **THEN** will not be taken is if A\$ does not equal YES and A is not less than 34.

You might like to type in the program below and RUN it several times to see how different values of A and A\$ determine what happens:

```
  5 PRINT "INPUT A NUMBER"
 10 INPUT A
 15 PRINT "INPUT A STRING"
 20 INPUT A$
 30 IF A$ = "YES" OR A < 35 THEN GOTO 200
 75 PRINT "CONDITION NOT MET"
100 STOP
200 PRINT "CONDITION MET"
```

Then change line 30 to:

```
 30 IF A$ = "YES" AND A < 35 THEN GOTO 200
```

RUN the program several more times using different values for A\$ and A. Do you see how **AND** and **OR** work? It should be noted that **OR** can be used with more than two conditions.

IF A = 1 **OR** B = 2 **OR** C = 3 **THEN PRINT** "EVERYTHING CHECKS OUT" – If at least one of the conditions (A = 1 or B = 2 or C = 3) is met the action after **THEN** will be carried out.

There is one more twist to the use of the logical conditions **OR** and **AND** in an **IF THEN** statement. You can combine **AND** and **OR** conditions in one **IF THEN** statement. Here is an example:

IF A = 1 **AND** B = 2 **OR** C = 3 **THEN PRINT** "SOMETHING WORKS" – If A equals 1 and B equals 2, the action after **THEN** will be executed; if C equals 3 (regardless of what A and B equal), the action after **THEN** will be executed.

When you use **AND** and **OR** together you can specify that two or more conditions be met (**AND**) or even if those conditions are not met if another set of conditions is met the actions will be executed (**OR**). You can create a variety of very complicated conditions with **AND** and **OR**.

The "**NOT**" operator is much less interesting or useful than **AND** and **OR**. **NOT** simply negates the conditional:

IF **NOT** A = 1 **THEN GOTO** 120 – If A is not equal to 1 then the computer proceeds to line 120 and begins executing the instructions there.

The instruction above is the same as **IF** A < > 1 **THEN GOTO** 120. Thus **NOT** generally duplicates an instruction that can be given in a different way.

There are several advanced programming concepts which involve the use of logical operators that have not been covered. They are, however, used less frequently than the concepts presented and they are best approached after you clearly understand the basic uses of logical operators.

FOR NEXT, and STEP

You have already used several simple **FOR NEXT** loops in Chapter 6. The program listed below will be used to illustrate some of the finer points of **FOR NEXT** loops:

```
10 PRINT "DOLLARS TO INVEST YEARLY"
20 INPUT D
30 PRINT "YEARS TO INVEST"
40 INPUT Y
50 PRINT "RATE OF INTEREST"
60 INPUT R
70 LET R = R/100
80 PRINT "YEAR        INVEST        TOTAL"
```

Note: type in 7 spaces between YEAR and INVEST and 7 spaces between INVEST and TOTAL.

```
 90 LET B = 1 + R
100 PRINT 1;TAB 11;D;TAB 24;D
110 FOR L = 1 TO Y
120 LET B = B*(1 + R)
130 LET S = (D*(B – 1))/R
```

140 **IF** L < Y **THEN PRINT** L + 1;**TAB** 11;(L + 1)*D;**TAB**
    24;**INT** S
200 **NEXT** L

Type in the program exactly as it is listed above. Most of the
key words used in the program will be familiar to you. Remember that the key word **TAB** in lines 100 and 140 is obtained by
holding down SHIFT and pressing the ENTER key to get an
inverse-F or function cursor. Then press the P key to get the
key word **TAB**. The same procedure is used to get the function
INT which is used in line 140. The **INT** function is associated
with the R key. If you try to type in **TAB** or **INT** by typing the
letters T A B or I N T the program will not work correctly.

This program lets you indicate how much money you will
invest per year, how many years you will invest that amount,
and the interest rate you will receive. The computer takes that
information and computes the accumulated investment per
year (under INVEST) and the total value (including accumulated interest) of your investment (under TOTAL). The amount
under TOTAL is rounded to whole dollars by the **INT** key word
(you'll learn how **INT** works later in this chapter).

RUN the program using 600 for the Dollars Invested per
Year, 10 for the Years to Invest, and 9 for the Rate of Interest.
Here is what you should get as a printout:

Table 7-1   Run of Investment Program

DOLLARS TO INVEST YEARLY
600
YEARS TO INVEST
10
RATE OF INTEREST
9

YEAR	INVEST	TOTAL
1	600	600
2	1200	1253
3	1800	1966
4	2400	2743
5	3000	3590
6	3600	4514
7	4200	5520
8	4800	6617
9	5400	7812
10	6000	9115

Thus, if you invest $600 a year for ten years you will end up
with $9115 of accumulated interest and principle. Lines 110 to
200 define a LOOP. This is the heart of the program since it
computes the amount of money that will be earned and prints
the results. It is called a loop because it is used several times,
once for each year you plan to invest. The **FOR NEXT** statement is used to control how many times the computer moves
through the loop. The **NEXT** in line 200 defines the lower
boundary of the loop. When the computer comes to a **NEXT** it
returns to the line where **FOR** occurs and goes through the
loop again. The way **FOR** operates is a little complicated. In
this case, L is the "control" variable in the loop (there is no
significance to the label L, it could be any other acceptable
variable name). The expression on the other side of the equals
sign tells the computer where to start and how many times to
run through the loop. Line 110 sets L equal to 1 (the initial value
for the first loop). Each time the computer runs through the
loop it increases the value of L by one. When L is equal to Y (the
final value), it goes through the loop one more time and moves
on to the line immediately after the **NEXT** statement. Y is the
number of years you plan to invest your money, so there will be
one line of results for each year you invest. Since in this
program there is no line after line 200 where **NEXT** appears,
the computer stops when it finishes the **FOR NEXT** loop.
As usual there are a few fine points that have not yet been
covered. Look at the **FOR NEXT** loop below (you may want to
SAVE the investment program before typing in the one below):

```
10 PRINT "HOW MUCH MONEY DO YOU WANT"
20 PRINT "TO INVEST FOR FIVE YEARS?"
30 INPUT H
40 PRINT "INTEREST RATE","PRIN + INTEREST"
50 FOR I = 7 TO 12 STEP .5
60 LET R = M*(1 + I/100)**5
65 REM TO GET **, HOLD DOWN SHIFT AND PRESS THE
   H KEY.
70 PRINT I,R
80 NEXT I
```

There is a new twist to this one. In its standard form, the
control variable in a **FOR NEXT** loop will be increased by one
each time the loop is used. This program, however, is designed
to print information on how much money will be accumulated

if a certain amount of money (M) is invested for five years at several different interest rates. We do not want the loop to increase the interest (I) by one each time. A more detailed breakdown is required. By adding the comment "**STEP** .5" it is possible to tell the computer to increase I by only .5 rather than one. A run of the program will illustrate what happens. (Replace the .5 with a 2 and the printout will begin with an interest rate of 7 percent and give data for rates of 9 and 11 percent.) Table 7-2 illustrates the output you should get if you type in line 50 **FOR** I = 7 **TO** 12 **STEP** .5. The interest rate is set initially at seven, and each time the loop is used the rate is increased by .5 until the final value of 12 is reached.

Table 7-2   Run of Investment Program with STEP .5

HOW MUCH MONEY DO YOU WANT?	
TO INVEST FOR 5 YEARS	
1000	
INTEREST RATE	PRINCIPAL AND INTEREST
7	1402.5517
7.5	1435.6393
8	1469.3281
8.5	1503.6567
9	1538.624
9.5	1574.2387
10	1610.51
10.5	1647.4568
11	1685.0582
11.5	1723.3534
12	1762.3417

Now what if you replace line 50 with this:

50 **FOR** I = 12 **TO** 7 **STEP** − .5

If you ran the program with this version it would begin with an interest rate of 12 and print results for 11.5, 11. 10.5 . . . and so on until the lowest acceptable value for I (7) is reached. The results of this version are shown in Table 7-3.

Another common variation for **FOR NEXT** loops is to put one inside another. The details of how this works are given in most books on BASIC. If you are using a program that has these *nested loops* the main thing to remember is to be sure the **NEXT** statements are in the proper order. In essence, a loop inside another loop will run through its entire range every time the outside loop runs through one step.

Table 7-3   Run of Investment Program with STEP −.5

HOW MUCH MONEY DO YOU WANT?	
TO INVEST FOR 5 YEARS	
1000	
INTEREST RATE	PRINCIPAL AND INTEREST
12	1762.3417
11.5	1723.3534
11	1685.0582
10.5	1647.4468
10	1610.51
9.5	1574.2387
9	1538.624
8.5	1503.6567
8	1469.3281
7.5	1435.6293
7	1402.5517

GOSUB RETURN

FOR NEXT loops let you use the instructions inside the loop over and over, the number of times they are used is determined by the control values provided. This is a very handy procedure. You will find **FOR NEXT** loops used in many programs.

Another handy procedure that is common in BASIC programs is the *subroutine*. A subroutine is a set of instructions that is used at several points in a program. The example program below will make the concept of a subroutine clearer:

```
10 GOSUB 100
20 PRINT "GUESS MY NUMBER"
30 INPUT G
40 GOSUB 200
50 GOTO 20
100 REM RANDOM NUMBER GENERATOR
110 RAND 0
120 LET N = INT (RND*100)
```

```
130 RETURN
200 REM GUESS CHECKING ROUTINE
210 IF G > N THEN PRINT "TOO HIGH TRY AGAIN"
220 IF G < N THEN PRINT "TOO LOW TRY AGAIN"
230 IF G = N THEN GOTO 280
240 GOTO 300
280 PRINT "GREAT, YOU GOT IT"
285 PRINT "I WILL THINK OF A NEW NUMBER"
290 GOSUB 100
300 RETURN
```

This program will print GUESS MY NUMBER at the top of the screen. You then type in a number between 0 and 100 and press ENTER. The computer compares your guess with the number it has generated and tells you if your guess is high, low, or correct. If it is high or low the computer tells you to try again and asks you to make another guess (don't forget to press ENTER). When you guess the number, the computer tells you GREAT, YOU GOT IT. Then it says I WILL THINK OF A NEW NUMBER and asks you to input another guess. To stop playing this game you should use the key word **STOP** followed by ENTER when the computer is waiting for you to input a number.

This program begins with the instruction **GOSUB** 100 in line 10. The key word **GOSUB** tells the computer to stop executing instructions sequentially. Instead it is to go to a subroutine which begins at the line number which follows **GOSUB**. In this case the subroutine begins on line 100. Actually line 100 contains a remark (**REM** statement) that tells us what the subroutine does. It generates a random number. The subroutine includes lines 100 to 130. We know line 130 is the end of the subroutine because it contains the key word **RETURN**. **RETURN** tells the computer that the subroutine has been executed. The computer then returns to the instruction just after the **GOSUB** key word. In this case, it is line 20. The computer has branched to a subroutine that did a particular task and then returned to continue normal execution of the program. Line 20 prints GUESS MY NUMBER; line 30 waits for you to type in a number. When you press ENTER the computer takes the number you typed in and assigns it to the variable named G (for guess).

Now we come to line 40 where there is another **GOSUB**, this time to line 200. The subroutine includes lines 200 through

300. This subroutine compares the number generated by the computer (variable N) with your current guess (variable G) and gives you either a hint or a congratulatory message. If you are incorrect the **GOTO** in line 240 sends the computer to line 300 which contains a **RETURN** statement. The computer returns to the instruction just beyond the **GOSUB** instruction that brought it to the subroutine. That is line 50 which contains another **GOTO** statement. It sends the computer back to line 20. The computer tells you to GUESS MY NUMBER and looks for more input. When you type in another number the computer comes to the **GOSUB** 200 instruction in line 40 once more, and things start all over again.

What happens if you guess the number correctly? Line 230 in the subroutine identifies the guess as correct and the instruction **GOTO** 280 is executed. The computer offers praise in 280 and tells you it will think of a new number to guess in line 285. Then line 290 does something interesting. We are already in a subroutine, but there is another **GOSUB** in 290. The **GOSUB** there sends the computer to the random number generator subroutine beginning in line 100. When the computer has a new number for variable N, it returns to the instruction just past the **GOSUB** instruction in 290. That is line 300 which is another **RETURN**. This time the computer goes back to line 50 because line 40 sent it to this subroutine.

There are several advantages to the use of subroutines. You can write all the instructions to do a particular task in one place in the program and then use the **GOSUB** instruction anytime you need that task done. For many people, writing programs is easier if you break the job down into a series of subroutines. (One theory of programming, however, criticizes the use of subroutines. The theory says that a program should be written so that it executes sequentially, from top to bottom, with no jumping around from one place to another.) In addition, when you must do a particular task at several points in the program, it is very easy to put a **GOSUB** at the appropriate place and avoid writing the same set of instructions at several points in the program.

PLOT and **UNPLOT.** Chapter 3 contained some examples of how the graphics symbols on the keyboard can be used to create figures on the video display. The TS1000 has another method for generating graphics on the video display. This method uses two new key words, **PLOT** and **UNPLOT.** Type in the following lines and observe what happens on the screen (press ENTER after each line):

PLOT 0,0   A dark square should appear in the bottom left corner of the screen.

PLOT 62,0   A dark square should appear in the bottom right corner of the screen.

PLOT 0,43   A dark square should appear in the top left corner of the screen.

PLOT 62,43   A dark square should appear in the top right corner of the screen.

These instructions should put small dark squares in the corners of the television screen. If one or more of the squares does not appear, it may be because the bezel around your television screen prevents you from seeing material at the extremes. Sometimes there are adjustments on the television that let you center the picture better; sometimes there is an adjustment that lets you reduce the size of the picture and thus pull the edges in a bit, and sometimes there is nothing you can do but avoid using graphics that get into that area of the display.

The **PLOT** and **UNPLOT** key words divide the video screen into forty-four lines numbered 0 to 43 from bottom to top. The second number after **PLOT** (or **UNPLOT**) tells the computer on which line the little square should go. Each of the forty-four **PLOT/UNPLOT** lines on the screen is also divided into 64 positions numbered 0 (far left) to 63 (far right). The first number after **PLOT** (or **UNPLOT**) tells the computer which position should be used. Figure 7.1 illustrates the screen layout for **PLOT** and **UNPLOT**. Those little dark squares that showed up when you used the **PLOT** instructions are called *pixels* which is short for picture elements. A pixel is the smallest element you can display on the screen. The general format for the **PLOT** instruction is:

PLOT position #, line #

The position number is called the X coordinate in most books while the line number is called the Y coordinate. Here is a program that illustrates the use of **PLOT**:

```
10 FOR X = 0 TO 63
20 PLOT X,21
30 NEXT X
```

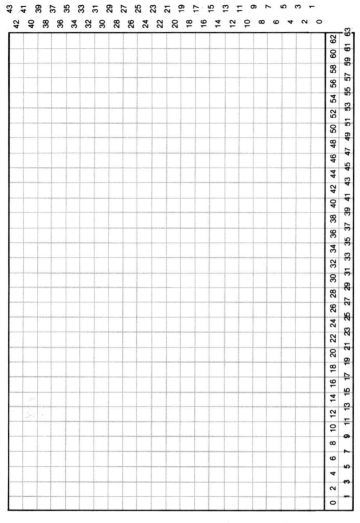

Figure 7.1 Screen map for **PLOT** and **UNPLOT** statements.

When you RUN this program it will draw a dark line across the middle of the screen (on line 21 from position 0 to position 63).

Here is another, more complicated program using graphics:

```
 5 LET Y = -1
10 FOR X = 0 TO 63
20 LET Y = Y + 1
30 PLOT X,Y
40 NEXT X
```

RUN this program and it will place a ragged diagonal line across the screen that starts at the bottom left and ends a few inches from the top right edge. You will also get a B/30 report. The B error code, in this instance, means the value of Y was larger than 43. There are only 43 lines available on the screen (0 is at the bottom, 43 is at the top) and you cannot tell the computer to **PLOT** on a line with a number greater than 43 because such a place doesn't exist on the screen. Type in:

> **PRINT** Y

and press ENTER. The computer should print the number 44 on the screen. Now modify line 20 as follows:

> 20 **IF** Y < 43 **THEN LET** Y = Y + 1

RUN the program again. This time the line snakes up the screen until it reaches line 43 at the top. The value of Y will not increase each time the value of X increases. That means the line will continue to move across the screen, but it will be on the same line (line 43). Now add another line of instructions to the program:

> 25 **IF** X > 0 **THEN UNPLOT** X − 1, Y − 1

The key word **UNPLOT** works just like **PLOT** except that it erases the little dark square on the screen. Line 25 tells the computer to **UNPLOT** or erase the area of the screen that is just below and just to the left of the spot where the **PLOT** instruction in line 30 is operating. RUN this version of the program. One little square seems to walk up the screen until it reaches the top. Then a solid line appears. Why didn't **UNPLOT** in line 35 erase the line at the top? Because when Y equals 43 the **PLOT** instruction begins working only on line 43, but the **UNPLOT** instruction never does anything to line 43 because 1 is always subtracted from Y. That means **UNPLOT** will be trying to erase line 42 (Y − 1) while **PLOT** draws on line 43.

Here is a program that uses **PLOT** to place random dots on the screen:

```
10 LET Y = INT (RND*43)
20 LET X = INT (RND*63)
30 PLOT X,Y
40 GOTO 10
```

RUN this program to see how it works; press **BREAK** when you've seen enough.

The program below lets you draw figures on the screen:

```
 10 LET X = 0
 20 LET Y = 0
 25 LET P = 1
 30 IF P = 1 THEN PLOT X,Y
 35 IF P = 0 THEN UNPLOT X,Y
 40 IF INKEY$ = "5" THEN LET X = X − 1
 50 IF INKEY$ = "8" THEN LET X = X + 1
 60 IF INKEY$ = "6" THEN LET Y = Y − 1
 70 IF INKEY$ = "7" THEN LET Y = Y + 1
 80 IF INKEY$ = "W" THEN LET P = 0
 90 IF INKEY$ = "Q" THEN LET P = 1
 95 IF P = 0 THEN PLOT X,Y
100 GOTO 30
```

This program lets you **PLOT** figures on the screen in much the same way that Etch-A-Sketch works. When you RUN the program a small dark square will appear in the bottom left corner of the screen. If you press any of the arrow keys (the 5, 6, 7, and 8 keys) a dark line will be drawn in the direction of the arrow you pressed. If you want to move without leaving a trail press the **UNPLOT** key (the W key). Now when you press the arrow keys a flashing dot shows you where you are on the screen, but no line is drawn as it moves. To return to the standard mode where a line is drawn, press the **PLOT** key (the Q key). Although this program is relatively short it can entertain the kids for hours. When you want to stop execution of the program, press the **BREAK** key. To erase the screen so you can start again, press **BREAK**, then press ENTER, and RUN the program again.

As the program stands now you can get an error report if you run off the top of the screen. You can add additional instructions that prevent that:

```
75 IF Y < 0 OR Y > 43 OR X < 0 OR X > 63 THEN GOTO
   10
```

Line 75 tests the values of X and Y to see if either is outside the boundary values of the screen. If either one is then the computer jumps to line 10. That will reset the program so that it is in the **PLOT** mode and the cursor is in the bottom left corner of the screen. Remember, however, that the more instructions and checks you add to a program such as this, the slower it will work. In addition, you cannot run this program in the **FAST** mode because the program will continually execute instructions and never have time to attend to the video display.

SUBSCRIPTED VARIABLES

We now come to one of the last major concepts in BASIC, subscripted variables. As noted earlier, variables have names (A, A4, A$, AA, etc.), and they have values. There are two major types of variables – string and numeric, and BASIC has several instructions that work only on either numeric or string variables.

Up to this point we have dealt with simple variables with names that are not, so far as the computer is concerned, related. Variables such as A1 and A2 or TEST1 and TEST2 are just variables to the computer; the similarity of the names means nothing to it. There are no special instructions, for example, that will let you deal with all the variables that have TEST in their name (e.g., TEST1, TEST2, TEST3). BASIC does, however, provide a means of dealing with groups of variables. You do it through the use of "subscripted" variables.

Variables with names like A, TEST, and TOTAL3 are just plain, garden variety variables. Variables with names like A(1), TEST(1), and TOTAL(3) are a different matter. The variable A4 is simple a convenient name. A(4), on the other hand, is a "subscripted" variable; A is the variable name and 4 is the subscript. If you think of the data in a computer as a parade then A4 might be one lone clown who marches by. A(4), on the other hand, might be one rider in a row of riders. The rider on the far right of the row of riders might be A(1), the one next would be A(2), the next A(3), and the one on the far left would be A(4). If these riders were data in a computer they would be called a *list* or *one dimensional array* since they are an associated group arranged along one dimension.

Now suppose a band comes marching by. Instead of one row, a band is made up of a *matrix* or *array* of people arranged in rows and columns. The person in the first row and first column might be given the variable name B(1,1) while a tuba player in the fifth row and eighth column would be B(5,8). To the computer, the double subscripts in the variable names for the band represent the column and row placement of the variables. This is a handy procedure when you have to deal with a large number of variables that are related to one another in some systematic way. In BASIC there are ways of dealing with subscripted variables that cannot be used with regular variables. (It is important, however, to keep in mind that a subscripted variable such as A(2) is an entirely different variable from A2 and A$(2). A$(2) is, of course, a string variable with a single subscript.) Here is an example that illustrates the use of subscripted variables:

```
10 PRINT "HOW MANY TOOK THE TEST?"
20 INPUT T
25 DIM S(T)
30 FOR X = 1 TO T
40 PRINT "TYPE IN SCORE ";X;", PRESS ENTER"
50 INPUT S(X)
60 NEXT X
65 LET TOTAL = 0
70 FOR Y = 1 TO T
80 LET TOTAL = TOTAL + S(Y)
90 NEXT Y
100 LET MEAN = TOTAL/T
110 PRINT "THE MEAN SCORE ON THE TEST"
120 PRINT "WAS ";MEAN
```

This little program lets you type in the students' scores from a test. It uses the subscripted variables S(#) to store the scores. The first thing the program does is ask you how many scores there are. You input that as the value for variable T in line 20. If T equals 3, that means there must be room in the computer for three scores which, in the program, will be stored as S(1), S(2), and S(3). Line 25 uses a new key word, **DIM**, to tell the computer that you plan to use a subscripted variable named S later in the program and that it will have 3 values. (If you tell the computer that there will be 24 scores, then line 25 will set variable S up for 24 different subscripts – S(1) through S(24).)

If you use subscripted variables in a program you must use the **DIM** instruction to tell the computer what to expect before the subscripted variable is used. **DIM** is short for dimension. It tells the computer to set aside a section of memory that will be used to store the values of each element of the subscripted variable.

There is a **FOR NEXT** loop in lines 30 through 60 of the program. The first time through this loop the computer asks you to type in the first test score and it assigns that score as the value of S(1). The second time through the loop, it gets the value for S(2), and so on. The other **FOR NEXT** loop in the program is in lines 70 through 90. That loop adds up all the scores on the test and puts the total in the variable named TOTAL.

Finally, the computer divides TOTAL by the number of scores and prints out the average or mean score on the test. This program illustrates one of the major advantages of subscripted variables. They allow you to use **FOR NEXT** loops to get values assigned to the correct variables.

The subscripted variable in the test scoring program is a one dimensional variable. The TS1000 will let you define or dimension (**DIM**) as many one dimensional variables as you like, each with whatever number of subscripts needed. **DIM** R(345), for example, sets aside enough memory for 345 variables named R(1) through R(345). There is, however, one limitation. You must have the memory available to set aside. If you don't, the computer will tell you there is a "B" error. In addition, even if you do have enough memory at the beginning of a program for many dimension instructions you may not have enough memory to do all that dimensioning, store the program, run the video display, and execute the program. Keep in mind how much memory you have available as you work with **DIM**.

Remember, also, that **DIM** can be used to set up multiple dimensional arrays or matrixes as well as one dimensional subscripted variables. **DIM** R(2,4) sets aside enough memory for a variable that has 2 rows and 4 columns:

| R(1,1) | R(1,2) | R(1,3) | R(1,4) |
| R(2,1) | R(2,2) | R(2,3) | R(2,4) |

DIM AND STRING VARIABLES

Thus far we have been dealing with numeric subscripted variables. Do string variables work the same way? Almost. If you give the instruction **DIM** A$(26), the computer will set aside enough memory for string A$ which can have 26 characters. A$, for example, could have a value of "ABCDEFGHIJKL MNOPQRSTUVWXYZ." Try this little demonstration program:

```
10 DIM A$(26)
20 LET A$ = "ABCDEFGHIJKLMNOPQRSTUVWXYZ"
30 FOR X = 1 TO 26
40 PRINT A$(X)
50 NEXT X
```

RUN this program and it will print the letters A through W down the left side of the screen. Press CONT and ENTER, and the computer will type the rest of the alphabet (it ran out of room after typing W) through Z. Each of the values of the subscripted variables A$(#) is one of the letters in the 26 character string. Now, delete line 10 (just type 10 and press ENTER). RUN the program again. It does the same thing whether the DIM instruction is in the program or not. Thus the DIM instruction is required for a one dimensional numeric array, but not for a one dimensional string array. In some programs it is a good idea to dimension string arrays anyway since the computer sets aside the memory it will need for the string. If you don't, it is possible that a long string that is needed late in the program will overtax your memory capacity and stop program execution. The sooner you realize you don't have enough memory the sooner you can try to rewrite the program to conserve memory.

What about multidimensional string arrays? What does DIM A$(4,3) mean? It means the computer is to set aside memory space for four different strings, each of which can have 3 characters. It might work like this:

```
10 DIM A$(4,3)
20 FOR X = 1 TO 4
30 INPUT A$(X)
40 NEXT X
50 FOR Y = 1 TO 4
60 PRINT A$(Y)
70 NEXT Y
```

RUN this program and input the strings CAT, DOG, HIM, and HER when the computer looks for input in the first FOR NEXT loop. The computer will accept the four strings (CAT,

DOG, HIM, HER) and then print each of them on the screen in the second **FOR NEXT** loop. In this program A$(1) will equal CAT, A$(2) will equal DOG, and so on. With a numeric variable that has multiple subscripts you could not access a whole row at once, but that is perfectly acceptable with strings. For example, if you **DIM** A(4,2), then **LET** A(1,1) equal 2 and **LET** A(1,2) equal 4, you cannot then expect A(1) to equal 24. With a string, however, it works just like that.

After you run the program above, type in **PRINT** A$(1,1) and press ENTER. You should get a C on the screen since C is the first letter in the first string of this array. **PRINT** A$(1,2) will place an A on the screen since it is the second letter in CAT. Here is a summary of the matrix that makes up A$(#,#) in the example program:

A$(1,1)=C	A$(1,2)=A	A$(1,3)=T
A$(2,1)=D	A$(2,2)=O	A$(2,3)=G
A$(3,1)=H	A$(3,2)=I	A$(3,3)=M
A$(4,1)=H	A$(4,2)=E	A$(4,3)=R

If you tell the computer that all the strings in the A$ matrix will be 3 characters long and then give it HELLO as one of the strings, the computer will accept it, but when you ask for that string later all that will be stored there will be HEL. In addition, if you tell the computer the string will be 3 characters long and then give it a two character string, the string will be filled out with spaces up to the maximum number of characters you said would be in the string.

Note that we have only used single letter names for the string arrays. TS1000 BASIC lets you use long names for regular strings (e.g., TEST), but you are limited to single letter names in subscripted string variables as well as subscripted numeric variables. The most complex array that we have used so far has been a two dimensional one. You are not limited to two dimensions. A three dimensional array, for example, could be used to represent each of the small cubes in a Rubik's Cube.

FUNCTIONS IN TS1000 BASIC

The final aspect of BASIC that we will discuss is functions. A function is much like canned laughter on a TV program. Whenever the producer needs laughter,   pushing the right button will produce it. Functions work the same way. If you need the square root of a number, for example, you could write a subroutine that uses several BASIC key words to do the job. There is, however, a function in TS1000 BASIC that does the job for you. The instruction **LET** M =**SQR** A will take the square root of A and assign that value to variable M. If A equals 81, the M will equal 9. If you type **PRINT SQR** 81 and press ENTER the computer will print the answer 9 on the display. To get the key word **SQR** you must hold down the SHIFT key and press ENTER. That changes the cursor to an inverse-F cursor. Then you look for **SQR** and find it under the M key. Pressing M will produce the **SQR** key word if you have an inverse-F cursor. Note that when you press **SQR** the cursor changes back to an inverse-L. You must hold down the SHIFT key and press EN-TER each time you need a function key word.

There are two families of functions, one that works with numeric variables and one that works with string variables. You have already used several numeric functions in example programs (e.g., **INT** and **RND**). Here is a summary of the numeric functions available in TS1000 BASIC:

SQR A – gives the square root of A. A must be a positive number, but it can be a variable (**SQR** A), a number (**SQR** 56), or an expression such as **SQR** (X/2*3.5). Most functions will work with variables, numbers (or strings), and expressions.

ABS A – gives the absolute value of A. That is, whether X is positive or negative, **ABS** X is always positive. If A equals − 5, **ABS** A will equal + 5. If A equals + 5, **ABS** A will again equal + 5. A can be a variable (**PRINT ABS** A), a number (**LET** A = **ABS** − 5), or an expression such as **LET** B = **ABS**(A − 4*6).

INT A – finds the integer or whole number part of a number. In TS1000 BASIC, regardless of whether the number is positive or negative, **INT** chops off everything to the right of the decimal. **PRINT INT** 12.3 would produce 12 while **PRINT INT** 12.9 also produces 12. **PRINT INT** − 7.1 and **PRINT INT** − 7.7 both produce 7.

PI – The **PI** symbol under the M key is the same as the value of Π. **PRINT PI** will produce 3.1415927.

SGN A – IF A is greater than 0, then **SGN** A will equal 1, and if A is a negative number then **SGN** A will equal −1. The instruction **LET** M = **SGN** B will set M equal to 0 if B equals 0, −1 if B is a negative number, and +1 if B is a positive number. **LET** N = **SGN** (B − C + X) will set N equal to 0, +1, or −1 depending on the value of the expression (B − C + X). **SGN** is short for sign.

RND – This function is used to generate a random number between 0 and 1. The numbers generated will never be 0 or 1. Instead, they will be decimal numbers between 0 and 1 such as .0011291504 or .78868103. You can use other key words to get numbers in any range you need. **LET** M = **INT** (**RND***11), for example, will set M equal to numbers between 0 and 10. **LET** M = (**INT**(**RND***10)) + 1 will set M equal to numbers between 1 and 10.

Another key word, **RAND** is also useful when generating random numbers (used most often in games). In some cases you may get the same pattern of numbers each time a game is run. If you add the key word **RAND** to the program at the point just before you use **RND**, the numbers generated will be different each time. There is an example of the use of **RAND** and **RND** earlier in the chapter.

Trigonometric Functions

TS1000 BASIC has a whole set of functions that deal with trigonometric values in radians. **PRINT COS** 34, for example, produces − 0.84857027. Here are the trig functions available:

    COS – cosine   **ARCCOS** – arccosine   **SIN** – sine
ARCSINE – arcsine   **ARCTAN** – arctangent **TAN** – tangent

The **EXP** function returns the natural antilog of the value which follows **EXP**. **PRINT EXP** 4 produces 54.59815. The **LN** function returns the natural log of the value which follows **LN**. **PRINT LN** 4, for example, produces 1.3862944.

Two more numeric functions, **PEEK** and **USR** are explained in Chapter 8.

NOTE: In Chapter 6 the priority system used by TS1000 BASIC was described. The computer does multiplication before addition unless you have changed the priority order by adding parentheses to math expressions. The math functions described above have the highest priority. Functions are calculated even before multiplication and division.

String Functions

One string function, **INKEY\$** has already been discussed in Chapter 6. There are five other functions that work with strings:

CHR$ # – To explain this function we must first deal with the character code the computer uses. The TS1000 cannot store the letter A or the key word **PRINT** in memory. It is only capable of storing patterns of electrical charges that represent numbers. The instructions that let the computer speak BASIC also include a code pattern that assigns each letter, number, key word, and special character a number. When you type in the key word **INKEY$**, for example, the computer actually stores the number code for **INKEY$** in the memory of the computer. The number code for **INKEY$** is 65. The code for D is 41. The **CHR$** function lets you use the direct code for a character or a key word. Type in **PRINT CHR$** 41 and press ENTER. A D appears on the screen. Type **PRINT CHR$** 65 and press ENTER. You should get the key word **INKEY$**. The **CHR$** function lets you use the code numbers normally used internally by the computer. Numbers 0 through 255 (except for 67 through 111 and 122 through 126) all have a symbol, letter, number, or key word associated with them in the TS1000 code. Here is a short program that will print out the code numbers and the characters or key words that go with them:

```
10 FOR X = 0 TO 255
20 PRINT X;
30 PRINT " IS CODE FOR",
40 PRINT CHR$ X
50 NEXT X
```

RUN this program and it will show you the characters associated with the numbers 0 through 21. Zero is the code for a space, so you won't actually see anything on the first line. Codes 1 through 10 are graphics symbols. They are followed by many other symbols. Press **CONT** and ENTER to see the characters for numbers 22 through 43. Continue to press **CONT** and ENTER to see the entire code pattern. (If you give the computer the instruction **FAST** before executing this program it will produce each page of codes faster, but it will blank the television screen while it is working.)

Remember that numbers 67 through 111 (and 122 through 126) do not have characters assigned to them. Thus the computer prints a ? when any of these numbers are used. In addition, codes 112 through 127 also produce question marks. That is because these codes are associated with keys that call for an action (e.g., the arrow keys, the ENTER, EDIT, DELETE, GRAPHICS, and FUNCTION keys).

From 128 to 255 the codes stand for graphics symbols, inverse characters (white character on black background), and key words in BASIC.

Using **CHR$** with **PRINT AT** or **TAB** enables you to print symbols, characters, even BASIC key words anywhere on the screen. The manual that comes with your computer contains an appendix that lists the codes and the symbols or key words associated with each code.

CODE – This string function lets you determine the code of the first letter in the string specified. If A$ equals CAT, then **PRINT CODE** A$ will produce 40 because 40 is the code for the letter C (the first letter in the string CAT).

LEN – This string function lets you determine how many characters (including spaces) are in a particular string. IF A$ equals CAT, then **PRINT LEN** A$ will produce 3 since there are three letters in CAT.

STR$ and **VAL**. In one of the example programs in Chapter 6 the point was made that you cannot perform math operations on strings nor can you perform string functions on numeric variables. Although this is generally true, there is a way of getting around these limitations using the **STR$** and **VAL** functions. **STR$** can be used to convert a numeric variable into a string variable, and **VAL** will convert a string variable into a numeric variable. Here is an example that shows how it works:

```
 5 PRINT "INPUT A"
10 INPUT A
15 PRINT "INPUT A$
20 INPUT A$
30 PRINT 2*A
40 PRINT 2*A$
```

You can input lines 10 through 30 with no problems, but the computer won't allow you to enter line 40 in the program. You are trying to perform an arithmetic operation on a string. Use the DELETE key to get rid of line 40 at the bottom of the screen. If you try to substitute the line below for the old line 40:

```
40 PRINT CODE A
```

you will find again that the computer will not accept it. You are trying to use a string function on a numeric variable. Use the

DELETE key to get rid of line 40. Now RUN the program (lines 10 through 30) and input the number 48 for variable A and 1234 for the string A$. Your screen should first display **INPUT** A (respond with 48 and press ENTER), then the display will reply **INPUT** A$ (respond with 1234). Then the computer will multiply A by 2 and print 96 on the screen.

Now add the following lines to the program:

```
40 LET B$ = STR$ A
50 PRINT CODE B$
60 LET B = VAL A$
70 PRINT B*2
```

Now RUN the program again giving A the value of 48 and A$ the value 1234. Just as before the computer prints 96 (2 times 48) from line 30. Line 40 converts the numeric variable A (which equals 48) to the string variable B$. Line 50 applies the string function **CODE** to B$ and produces a 32 on the screen. Why 32? Because the first character in B$ (and in A) is 4 and the code for 4 is 32. If you tell the computer to **PRINT CHR$** 32 the computer will print 4. If you tell the computer to **PRINT** B$ at this point it would print 48 because B$ now equals 48.

In line 60 the string A$ which equals 1234 is converted to the numeric string B. Line 70 multiplies B by 2 and prints the result which is 2468. Using **VAL** and **CHR$** you can convert string variables to numeric variables and vice versa.

What happens if you apply the **VAL** function to a string that is not made up of numbers? What if A$ equals TEST? This will produce an error. The computer cannot treat TEST as a number. However, there is a little twist to the plot:

```
10 LET TEST = 10
20 INPUT A$
30 LET B = VAL A$
40 PRINT B*2
```

This program will work if you tell the computer that A$ equals TEST because you have defined TEST as a numeric variable with the value of 10. Line 40 will multiply B by 2 and print 20 as the answer. This little trick, however, is likely to cause problems. You are better off sticking with the use of **VAL** only on strings that can directly represent numeric values.

At this point you may have a more general question about the usefulness of **VAL** and **CHR$**. Admittedly, they are not likely to show up in every single program you use. There are, however, occasions when they are useful. For example, in many programs you are asked to input a numeric value. If you make a mistake and input a character instead, the character input for a numeric variable may stop execution of the program. A better way to get input might be to tell the computer to expect a string input (but tell the user that a number is expected). Then if the operator inputs a letter or symbol instead of a number your program can check to see if it is a number. If it is a number, use the **VAL** function to convert the string to a numeric variable. If it is a character, print a message on the screen explaining what should be input and use a **GOTO** to get the input again.

This concludes the material on BASIC. As mentioned in Chapter 6 this is not intended to be a comprehensive introduction to BASIC that will prepare you to write your own programs. It is a good start in that direction, but it isn't enough. There are several other books that deal exclusively with programming in BASIC on the TS1000. Instead, these chapters were designed to give you enough knowledge about how BASIC works on the TS1000 to enable you to use published programs. You will find many books and magazines that contain programs written for the TS1000. The material in Chapters 6 and 7 should be enough to let you type those programs into your computer and use them. In many instances you should be able to troubleshoot them when problems occur and you will be able to modify and customize them so that they better meet your specific needs.

CHAPTER 8

Peeking and Poking Around

This is an optional chapter that provides a bit of information on the internal organization of the TS1000. None of the material in this chapter is absolutely essential for readers who plan to write or use programs written in BASIC. It will be useful to readers who want to write machine language programs or special BASIC programs. The chapter begins with an explanation of the memory map of the TS1000 and of two BASIC key words, **PEEK** and **POKE**. The BASIC key word **USR** is also introduced. The chapter also describes some important memory locations in the TS1000.

THE MEMORY MAP

The TS1000 computer uses the Z80 microprocessor chip which was designed by the Zilog Corporation. The Z80 chip is capable of addressing 64K of memory. Each K of memory can store 1024 characters; 64K is thus equivalent to 65536 storage locations with each location (called an address) capable of storing one character (called a byte). The ability to address memory simply means that the chip can select any one of the character storage locations in the computer's memory and read what is stored there or write new data to that byte of memory.

Microprocessor chips such as the Z80, Motorola's 6502 and the 6800 are all capable of addressing or using a maximum of 64K of memory. (Newer chips such as the Intel Corporation's 8088 can address much more memory.) When an engineer designs a computer he or she must take into consideration the organization of memory in the computer. Each computer has a *memory map* which indicates how the memory is used. The 64K of memory that can be addressed by the Z80 microprocessor chip can be used for three general purposes:

  1. ROM.   All computers must have some Read Only Memory which has been programmed at the factory. ROM contains the instructions needed to enable the components that make up the computer operate as an integrated system. In many computers today, ROM also contains the instructions the computer needs to understand programs written in a higher level computer language such as BASIC. The computer can read data from ROM, but it cannot change any data stored in ROM.

  2. RAM.   Random Access Memory is memory that can be used by the computer operator. You can store data or programs in it. The computer can read each byte of memory to determine what is stored there.

  3. Dedicated Addresses.   Each location in the memory map is given an address number (0 to 65535 in Z80 based computers). Thus when the microprocessor chip wants to read from or write to a particular byte or cell of memory it must send a signal to the memory that designates one of the 65536 locations. In the memory maps of most computers the great majority of memory addresses are actually connected (or can be connected) to computer memory, either RAM or ROM. In most systems, however, a few addresses are not connected to memory at all but to other devices such as the circuitry that makes a printer or the keyboard work. In such a system the Z80 chip may think it is reading a particular memory location when it is actually sensing which key on the keyboard has been pressed. The memory addresses used in such a manner are called *dedicated addresses*.

  Another type of dedicated memory involves the use of memory for a particular function. Many of the inexpensive computers set aside a portion of their memory map for operating the video display. A character written to some memory addresses ends up on the screen of the video display. This "memory mapped video" approach sets aside one byte of memory for each location on the video display. The codes stored in one section of memory determine what you see on the display.

The TS1000 Memory Map

  Table 8-1 shows you how the TS1000 uses the memory addresses available to it.

Table 8-1 Memory Map of TS1000

65535	Largest memory address usable on the TS1000.
32767	Last byte of memory actually installed if you have a 16K memory module.
18431	Last byte of memory if you have 2K of RAM.
17407	Last byte of memory if you have 1K of RAM.
16384	Memory from 16384 to 16508 is set aside for storing system variables.
16383	Last byte of empty ROM space. RAM starts at 16384.
8192	Space between 8192 and 16483 currently unused. ROM could easily be added here.
8191	Last byte of the ROM which contains the instructions for BASIC.
0	First byte of memory. The instructions that let you run BASIC take up the first 8K of ROM.

The TS1000 puts 8K of ROM in the memory map at addresses 0 to 8191. The ROM located there contains the instructions the computer needs to run the computer and to interpret programs written in BASIC.

Just above the 8K of ROM is a blank section of memory. Nothing is normally connected to the memory addresses from 8192 to 16383. Accessory manufacturers who want to put programs in ROM or who need dedicated addresses for their hardware could use addresses in this area.

The RAM memory used by this computer begins at memory address 16384. If you have only 1K of memory in your computer there will be RAM from 16384 to 17407. That is 1024 bytes of memory. The first 125 bytes (16384 to 16508 of RAM memory), however, are used for system variables. System variables will be explained in the next section. Over 700 bytes are needed to take care of the video display if you have a full screen

(24 lines of 32 characters). You can end up with less than 200 bytes of RAM which are actually available for writing BASIC programs.

If you have 2K of RAM memory (standard on the TS1000) well over a thousand bytes of memory are available for programming, and with the 16K memory module you have enough to write very long BASIC programs.

To summarize, the TS1000 puts its ROM at the bottom of the memory map, beginning at memory location 0. After 8K of ROM there is an 8K blank space in the memory map followed by at least 1K of RAM. As you can see there is plenty of room for expansion in this memory map since no more than 10K (8K ROM and one or two K of RAM) is used in the basic configuration.

Important Memory Locations

Several books, many much longer than this one, have been devoted to dissecting the contents of the TS1000's memory. We will, therefore, give you only a taste of what is stored in the RAM and ROM of the TS1000. There are hundreds of memory locations that perform a particular function that might be useful to a programmer. Some of these are part of the ROM which contains instructions for BASIC, and some are in RAM. Here is a list of a few memory locations and what they do:

7680 – 8191. These locations in ROM contain codes for the video display characters. The pattern for each character is stored in eight bytes. The characters on the video display are actually patterns of dots that create the desired letter or character. The computer works with a matrix of dots. The matrix is 8 lines of 8 dots each. The letter A, for example, is created by the following dot pattern:

```
0 0 0 0 0 0 0 0
0 0 1 1 1 1 0 0
0 1 0 0 0 0 1 0
0 1 0 0 0 0 1 0
0 1 1 1 1 1 1 0
0 1 0 0 0 0 1 0
0 1 0 0 0 0 1 0
0 0 0 0 0 0 0 0
```

The ones in the diagram above tell the computer to put a dot on the screen. Every character the computer can display has a dot matrix pattern in this section of ROM. Each of the lines of ones and zeros listed above can be stored in one byte of memory. (All data stored in RAM or ROM is actually stored as patterns of ones and zeros.) One byte of memory is made up of eight bits. A bit of computer memory can store one piece of data, and that data can be either 1 or 0. To be completely accurate, what we call ones and zeros are really the presence of an electrical signal (On equals 1) or the absence of a signal (Off equals 0). Thus the dot patterns for the video characters are stored in memory as eight bytes of data with each byte indicating the pattern of dots to be displayed on each of the eight lines in the dot matrix.

16384. This memory location is in the system variable area mentioned earlier. Numbers are stored here that the computer may need as it runs a program. This byte of memory contains the report code which indicates whether the computer has encountered an error or not. If an error is encountered the number indicates what type of error it is.

16288 and 16289. These two memory locations together contain the address of the last byte of RAM. The numbers stored there will depend on how much memory you have.

16390. Memory location 16390 contains a number that tells the computer which cursor is currently displayed (K, L, F, or G).

16394. If you have a program listed at the top of the screen this byte of memory contains the number of the line that has the program cursor displayed between the line number and the instructions on that line.

16418. The number stored here tells the computer how many lines are at the bottom of the screen. The number stored here is one more than the actual number of lines at the bottom of the screen.

PEEK AND POKE

These two key words are not that useful in uncomplicated BASIC programs, but they can be very handy when the programming gets tough. In addition, you must use them when writing and using machine language programs on this computer. To see how **PEEK** works type in the following program:

```
10 LET A = PEEK 16394
20 PRINT A
```

Now RUN the program with the program cursor (the one in the listing at the top of the screen) at line 20. You should get 20 at the top of the screen and 0/20 at the bottom. Now press the ENTER key and move the program cursor to line 10. (Use the arrow keys on the top row to do this.) Now RUN the program again. This time the display should have a 10 at the top and 0/20 at the bottom. This little program made the variable A equal to the number stored in memory location 16394. That location is used to store the line number of the program that contains the program cursor. If you simply typed in **PRINT PEEK** 16394 you would get the same results.

The **PEEK** function lets you look at any memory location, RAM or ROM, and find out what number is stored there. Now let's look at **POKE**. Type in the following program:

```
10 INPUT A
20 POKE 16417,A
30 PRINT PEEK 16417
```

Now RUN the program and type in a number between 0 and 255. You should see the number displayed at the top of the screen. The program takes the number you input and assigns it to the variable A. Then the **POKE** instruction in line 20 puts the value of A in the memory location specified by the first number following **POKE**. In this case the number was 16417. Finally, line 30 looks at memory location 16417 and prints whatever number is stored there. RUN the program again and use a different number. Again the number you type in should appear at the top of the screen. The memory location used in this demonstration program is an unused byte in the program variable area of RAM. You cannot **POKE** data into ROM and you must be very careful where you **POKE** in RAM. If you happen to poke a number into a memory location the computer uses, it may well affect how the computer operates. In many instances it will cause the computer to "crash." Crashes do not damage the computer physically, but you may have to switch the machine off to get it to work again. The standard format for a **POKE** instruction requires two numbers. The first is the memory address where the data is to be stored. It must be a valid RAM address number. The TS1000 will let you **POKE** a ROM location, but nothing will happen. The second number after **POKE** is the number to be stored in memory. It must be between 0 and 255.

If you still have the three line program in memory, type in the line below and press ENTER:

POKE 16510,5   and press ENTER

Did the line number 10 change to line number 5? The simple three line BASIC program is stored in RAM just above the system variable area. The line number for the first line of program instructions was in memory location 16510. Poking 05 into that location changed the line number. It is possible to modify aspects of a BASIC program by poking the correct memory location.

Here is one more program using **PEEK** that might be useful to you:

```
10 LET A = PEEK 16389*256 – 16384
20 PRINT "TOTAL RAM IS ";A
30 LET B = PEEK 16388 + 256*PEEK 16389
40 PRINT "TOP OF RAM IS ";B – 1
```

This program uses memory locations 16389 and 16388 to determine how much RAM memory is installed in the computer. If you multiply the number stored in memory location 16389 by 256 you will get the value of the first nonexistent memory location at the top of the memory map. In a 1K computer the number is 68. Thus 68 times 256 is 17408. The last memory location that actually contains RAM is 17407. Since RAM memory starts at 16384 you can subtract that number from the variable A in the program above and determine how much RAM you have. A 1K computer will report there is 1024 bytes of RAM available. A computer with a 16K memory module attached will report there are 16384 bytes of RAM available and that the top of RAM is 32767.

THE USR FUNCTION

This function is one way to work with a type of programming called *machine language* programming. The instruction **PRINT USR** 18000 tells the computer to go to memory location 18000 and begin executing a machine language program which is stored there. If you would like to know more about machine language programming with the TS1000 there are several books on the topic. As noted earlier in this chapter we have only lightly touched on the topics discussed here. Our advice is to get BASIC well in hand before tackling the material introduced here. A good working knowledge of BASIC forms a nice foundation upon which to build knowledge of other ways to write computer programs.

CHAPTER 9

Selecting Accessories for Your Computer

The TS1000 is a minimal computer at a minimal price. The low price prompted hundreds of thousands of people to buy the TS1000 as their first computer. Its limitations prompted hundreds of companies to design and manufacture accessories for the little computer that so many people own. This chapter explains what many of the accessories do, what they won't do, and points out some of the pitfalls and problems associated with buying accessories.

Please heed two caveats before reading this chapter. First, we have included prices when discussing specific products even though computer product prices are notoriously fickle. The prices listed are those in effect at the beginning of 1983. You may find some prices have increased and many have decreased by the time you decide to buy accessories. Second, suppliers of computer accessories are an odd assortment. Most companies do have good intentions, some provide prompt service and excellent quality, most eventually deliver products that will work. Exercise reasonable caution when spending your hard earned money, however, because there *are* a few crooks and a few totally incompetent entrepeneurs out there.

EXTRA MEMORY

The ZX81 computer has enough memory built in to store about 1000 characters of program instructions, video display information and/or data. The Timex 1000 can store a little over 2000 characters. Even 2000 is precious little memory. The Atari 400 computer, by contrast, comes standard with 16K of

RAM memory (16384 characters), and the Commodore 64 has 64K of RAM (65536 characters). Many TS1000 owners find, all too quickly, that the standard 1K or 2K of RAM in their computer is simply not enough. You can, however, add extra memory by buying a memory pack that plugs into the expansion port on the back of the computer. You can buy a 16K memory pack from either Sinclair or Timex.

Several British and American companies other than Sinclair and Timex also make memory expansion modules for the TS1000. The following companies sell 16K modules at the prices listed:

JRS Software, 19 Wayside Avenue, Worthing, Sussex BN13 3JU. $50. (0903-65691)

Memotech, 7550 West Yale Avenue, Suite 220, Denver, Colorado 80227. $50. (303-986-0016)

Microcomputers Plus Inc., 349 East Main St., Galesburg, Illinois 61401. $70. (309-342-9572)

Kayde Electronic Systems, The Conge, Great Yarmouth, Norfolk NR30 1PJ. $60. (0493-57867)

Byte-Back Company, Rt. 3, Box 147, Brodie Road, Leesville, South Carolina 29070. $70 assembled and tested, $60 kit with all parts, $20 kit with few parts.

KB Enterprises, 8211 Valdosta Avenue, San Diego, California 92126. $50.

Wisconsin Electronics, P.O. Box 332, Milton, Wisconsin 53563. $35 kit.

Apropos Technology, 350 N. Lantana Avenue, Suite 821, Camarillo, California 93010. $50.

data-assette, 56 S. 3rd Street, Oxford, Pennsylvania 19363. $60. (1-800-523-2909).

Dolphin Computer, P.O. Box 3046, Redwood City, California 94064. $50.

Artic Computing, 396 James Reckitt Avenue, Hull, HU8 OJA, England. £35.

Hunter, 1630 Forest Hills Drive, Okemos, Michigan 48864. $32 for an 8K kit you assemble. This RAM uses a battery backup system so you don't lose data in it when the computer is turned off.

The companies listed above all offer memory expansion products that plug onto the back of the computer. The products vary in quality and appearance as well as price. Some memory modules have a homemade look to them; others are professionally finished. Some don't work reliably, others work well. Because products change quickly, we won't give you a recommendation about where to buy your extra memory. The best buy today may be a poor one next month. In general, however, we would recommend you buy from companies with a track record and from those that provide street addresses and/or telephone numbers. Companies that only have post office box numbers may be quite legitimate, but some use box numbers as a means of keeping the buying public at a distance. If they fold their tents in the night and steal away (with your money) it is very difficult to trace them.

A number of companies also sell larger memory modules. You can even get a 64K RAM module from a few sources. That is more memory than most home computers have today! The typical 64K memory module cost around $180 when this was written while a 16K RAM model averaged $50. Do you need 64K? Most people will not. The TS1000 is very stingy with its memory. It stores BASIC key words such as **GOSUB, PRINT**, and **CLEAR** as one character. The TS1000 thus uses 1 character of memory storage for **PAUSE** while many other computers need 5 characters of space for the same key word. If, however, you use your TS1000 to write very long programs in BASIC, or if you use it for applications that take lots of memory (e.g., inventory control, mailing lists), 64K might be handy. There is also a bit of one-up-personship in telling your buddies that you have 64K of RAM on your TS1000 while they only have 32K in their PETs or 48K in their Ataris. A few companies that sell larger memory modules are listed below. If the company was listed above, only the name is given here:

Byte-Back. $140 kit, $155 assembled for 64K.
Memotech. $180 for 64K. Produced the first popular 64K add-on circuit and advertises the most.
JRS Software, $120 for 64K.
Dolphin Computer, $150 for 64K.

BETTER KEYBOARDS

If there is one virtually universal complaint that can be legitimately lodged against the TS1000, it is that the tiny plastic keyboard is hard to use. If you write long BASIC programs on the TS1000, a full size, standard computer keyboard is a boon.

Many companies offer add-on keyboard kits that can be attached to the TS1000. Some of the add-on keyboards simply slip over the existing keyboard and give you a slightly better target for your fingers. Most, however, are completely separate keyboards which must be attached to the TS1000 via a cable. Installation usually involves soldering several wires to specified locations on the TS1000 circuit board.

Standard keyboards greatly improve your typing speed when installed properly. There are, however, some problems. Many of the keyboard kits currently offered by mail use surplus keyboards that were not designed for the TS1000. These keyboards are often of very high quality. Their original cost may well have been over $200. The TS1000, however, makes heavy use of each of its keys. A key may be used for two BASIC key words, a graphics symbol, a letter, and a BASIC function. If you use a standard surplus keyboard you may well find the frustration of using a tiny membrane keyboard replaced by the frustration of trying to use a keyboard with only letters and numbers embossed on the keyboard. It is very difficult to memorize the exact location of each key word and graphics symbol. Although they are generally more expensive, we prefer keyboards that have been specifically prepared for the TS1000. Kayde Electronic Systems (The Conge, Great Yarmouth, Norfolk NR30 1PJ England, 0493-57867), for example, sells a very nice keyboard for $80 with a case or $56 without a case. All the symbols on the standard membrane keyboard are embossed on the top of the larger expansion keyboard. Synergistic Design (P.O. Box 411023, Chicago, Illinois 60641) also markets a specially designed keyboard with appropriate key labels. It costs $90.

Gladstone Electronics (1585 Kenmore Avenue, Buffalo, New York 14217, 1-800-833-8400) also has a nice keyboard for the computer that sells for $105 with a metal case. It has clear plastic removable keytops that allow you to insert legends under them. Gladstone supplies correct legends for the computer. There are also six extra or spare keys on the keyboard. No soldering is required to install the keyboard, and the TS1000 itself fits inside the keyboard case. An English company (Fuller Micro Systems, The ZX Centre, Sweeting Street, Liverpool 2, England) also sells a keyboard kit with TS1000 legends. The keyboard is $80 and requires no soldering for installation. In addition, the case for the keyboard has enough room to place the rest of the TS1000 inside. Using the Gladstone or Fuller keyboard makes for a neater, more convenient appearance since everything is in one enclosure.

If you consider $80 to $105 a bit much for a bigger keyboard when the computer didn't cost much more than that, you can purchase a surplus keyboard kit for less than $50. You may be able to get around the lack of legends on the keys by writing the key words and symbols on stick-on mailing labels cut to fit the front of the keys (or by making a copy of the keyboard legends from an advertisement and attaching these to the keys).

If you happen to have a spare keyboard lying around you may be able to connect it to your TS1000 by following the directions in an article by Robert Trelease (Keyboard/System Conversion) which appeared in the May/June, 1982 issue of *Sync* magazine.

Another popular accessory for the TS1000 is a keyboard beeper. When you use an unmodified TS1000 there is no way to tell whether you have pressed a key hard enough to register except to look at the screen and see if the letter or word you want has appeared. The necessity for glancing at the screen every time you press a key tends to slow things down and is distracting. The solution is a beeper. When installed, a beeper makes a little beep or chirp each time you press a key hard enough to register. Audiograph Co. (3584 Leroy, Ann Arbor, Michigan 48103) sells a chirper for $10. Burnett Electronics (1729 Woodland Avenue, #D, Palo Alto, California 94303) sells a beeper for $12.

PRINTERS

Although the method varies from model to model, most computers can be connected to a variety of printers. In essence, a computer sends a coded signal to the printer. That code is made up of a pattern of On and Off signals with On being signified by one voltage and Off being indicated by another. Each character the printer can print is assigned a special code. When the printer gets the code for an A it prints an A on the paper.

Virtually every computer except the TS1000 uses a standard code called ASCII or American Standard Code for Information

Interchange. Most printers are also designed to use the ASCII code. Since the TS1000 uses its own unique code, however, you cannot simply go out and buy a printer and expect it to work properly with the TS1000. Three factors must be considered when selecting a printer:

1. Interface circuits are required to correctly connect the printer to the computer.

2. The computer must use the same code as the printer OR the interface must translate computer code into printer code.

3. Unless specifically designed for the TS1000 there is little likelihood that a printer will reproduce the graphics characters used on the TS1000.

Sinclair and Timex offer a tiny little printer that connects directly to the TS1000. It uses the same code as the computer; it has a built-in interface, and it can produce graphics as well as letters and numbers. The best thing about this printer is its price (under $100). On the negative side is the narrow, specially treated paper it uses. The paper comes in rolls and resembles the paper used in small adding machines. Like the computer, the printer can print 32 characters on each line. It prints at around 50 characters a second which is relatively slow when compared to more expensive printers using the same technology. The characters are legible, but they are not crisp. We feel the little printer will be useful for printing out listings of programs, but it is not a general purpose printer. That is fine, however, because the TS1000 is not a general purpose computer.

Another company, CAI Instruments (P.O. Box 2032, Midland, Michigan 48540, 517-835-6145) also sells a little printer for the TS1000. It also uses adding machine type paper and costs under $100. It is not a pretty device but it does seem to work well. CAI Instruments also manufactures an I/O board. I/O stands for input/output. The $80 board lets you attach several types of devices, including printers, to the TS1000.

A third midget printer for the TS1000 is the MW-100 from Mindware, Inc. (70 Boston Post Road, Wayland, Massachusetts 01778). Like the other two printers mentioned above it is ready to connect to the TS1000. However, it prints only 16 characters on a line. That means a printout of a program will not look the same as the listing on your video screen since the TS1000 puts as many as 32 characters on a line. The MW-100 costs $120.

Most printers sold today use one of two interface formats, serial or parallel. Sometimes the term RS-232 or RS-232C is used instead of the term serial, and "Centronics compatible" often means the same thing as parallel. Memotech sells a serial interface for $140 and a parallel interface for $105. If you need additional technical information on serial and parallel interfaces you may want to refer to another dilithium Press book, *Peanut Butter and Jelly Guide to Computers* by Jerry Willis.

OTHER ACCESSORIES

It seems amazing to us that a $100 computer has spawned such a diverse and active industry with many manufactuers supplying equipment for the machine. We would estimate you could spend over $50,000 just to buy one of each of the accessories currently being sold for the TS1000.

In this section we will describe a few of the more interesting accessories not mentioned already.

MODEMS. A modem is a device that lets you connect your computer to other computers over the phone. Byte-Back Industries sells a modem for the TS1000 for $120. It allows you to connect up to popular information utilities such as The Source and Micronet. This particular modem also has a serial interface built in that allows you to connect a standard printer to the computer.

CONTROL INTERFACES. Several companies sell interface modules that let you use the computer as an environmental control unit or in industrial control applications. You can, for example, instruct the computer to turn on the lights in the house at dusk or water the plants in your greenhouse when the soil moisture level reaches a certain percentage. Some people also use the computer to run security systems. These are not simple "take it home and use it" applications. You must generally write your own computer program, design and wire up sensor and control devices, and interconnect the computer to the control interface. This is not a Saturday night project! If you would like more information on control applications of microcomputers you may want to consult the dilithium Press book, *Microcomputers for External Control Devices* by James Gupton, or *Using and Abusing Your Timex Sinclair Computer* by Robert Swarts.

Byte-Back has a control module for the TS1000 for $70 assembled.

EXPANSION BOARDS. The TS1000 has a small connector on the back of the computer where most accessories are attached. That connector gets very busy if you have several accessories plugged into one connector at the same time. A few devices let you "piggy-back" accessories. That is, one plugs into the computer, the second plugs into the first, and so on.

Another solution is to use an expansion board. These boards plug into the back of the TS1000 and provide room for plugging in several accessories at once. Most of the expansion boards also have their own power supplies since the one that runs the computer can barely support the extra power needed for one accessory, much less several. Computer Continuum (301 16th Avenue, San Francisco, California 94118, 415-752-6294) sells an expansion board for $60 in kit form. It has its own power supply, accepts up to six different accessories including memory modules, and can be firmly attached to the TS1000. Aerco (Box 18093, Austin, Texas 78760, 512-385-7405) also sells an expansion board. Their $80 device lets you put accessory boards in a small "card cage" that connects to the computer via a cable.

BATTERY BACKUP. For $55 you can get a battery power supply that runs the computer for 1 hour (Syncware Company, 4825 Elrovia Avenue, El Monte, California 91723). The same company sells other backup systems that run the computer for between ½ hour to 2 hours. Most of these operate by sensing when the regular power is lost and automatically switching to battery backup. If you have "dirty power," that is, power that is unreliable or unstable, you can also use the battery backup systems to run the computer without connecting it to the wall plug.

GRAPHICS AIDS. Although the TS1000 has some ability to create graphics, there are several companies that sell devices that expand that ability. Zodex (Easthill, Oakham, Massachusetts 01068), for example, has a $90 graphics module that permits programmers to create more detailed graphics with the TS1000. Memotech's graphics module is much more powerful, but sells for $150. With it you can create graphics displays on the screen that rival those produced by computers costing much more than the TS1000.

Quicksilva (95 Upper Brownhill Road, Maybush, Soton, Hants, England) also manufactures a high quality graphics board that lets you create excellent black and white graphics. The cost is around $160. It is also available in the U.S. from Sinclair Place (P.O. Box 2288, Redmond, Washington 98052). Quicksilva produces a number of products for the TS1000 including expansion boards, memory boards, a board that lets you create sound effects, and boards that let you use different sets of characters. You might want to write for their catalog or for a catalog from Sinclair Place.

ROM-PAC Applications (5921 Alhambre Court, Norcross, Georgia 30093, 404-921-4471) also manufactures a product useful for graphics. Their Character Cartridge costs around $30 and lets you display upper and lowercase characters in three different fonts as well as special graphics characters and symbols. Kayde Electronic Systems of England has a similar board ($60) that is preprogrammed with 450 additional graphics symbols you can use in your programs. It also permits you to create your own graphic symbols and use them in your programs.

LOADING AIDS

One of the most frustrating aspects of working with the TS1000 is its rather temperamental attitude toward loading and storing programs on cassette tapes. Several companies sell loading aids. R.H. Enterprises (1408 N. 4th Avenue E., Newton, Iowa 50208) has a $7 aid that plugs into the cable between the recorder and the computer. You adjust the volume on the recorder until the light glows at an appropriate brightness. This aid seems to be the same sort of device that is described in an article by E. Ross Helton in the March/April, 1982 issue of *Sync* magazine. If you are handy with a soldering gun you can build it for a few dollars.

A more sophisticated loading aid is sold by Edson Electronics (P.O. Box 15211, Tampa, Florida 33684). It costs $29 and provides a digital display of loading levels. D. Bruce Electronics (The Beacon, Blackhall Rocks, Cleveland TS27 4BH England, 0783-863612) sells a loading aid for just under £13.

If the hassles of loading standard cassette tapes are no longer bearable, CAI Instruments has a $100 "Widgitape" system that uses very reliable industrial tape cassettes instead of standard audio cassettes. In addition, several companies sell disk drive systems for the TS1000. The cost of disk drives, however, is many times the cost of the computer.

ORGANIZERS

The table or desk that houses your computer is likely to acquire a cluttered look rather quickly. Tapes are scattered about, cables run everywhere, and several manuals always seem to be in the wrong place. Ruskraft Engineering (P.O. Box 306, Tinley Park, Illinois 60477) makes a molded plastic computer organizer that has depressions that fit the computer and the tape recorder. Cables are run underneath the organizer and there is room for storing some accessories. At $17 it is an inexpensive way of uncluttering your computer installation.

The English manufacturer, Peter Furlong (Products Unit 5, South Coast Road Industrial Estates, Peace Haven, Sussex, England, 07914-81637) also sells an organizer. Called the ZX81 Work Station, this $40 product has provisions for placing the lip of your television on the edge of the work station so that it angles up a few degrees. The work station lets you conceal cables and store accessories conveniently. There is even a built-in on-off switch. The U.S. supplier is Jim Griner (P.O. Box 1, Princeville, Illinois 61559).

A FINAL WORD

The products described in this chapter are only a small sampling of those that are available. There are, however, sources of additional information. Many of those sources are described in the next chapter.

CHAPTER 10

Sources of Additional Information

We hope this book has served as a good beginning point, an introduction, to the use of your TS1000 and to the field of personal computing. Yet we have only scratched the surface. There is more, much more, to be learned about your computer and about personal computing. This final chapter will provide you with some clues about how to get the additional information you need.

MAGAZINES

SYNC. We feel this is an excellent magazine for owners of TS1000 computers. Published six times a year it is filled with hundreds of ads for new products and new software that runs on your computer. The articles range from introductory pieces for the beginner to descriptions of how to build accessories and papers on advanced programming topics. Subscriptions are around $20 a year. The U.S. address for *Sync* is 39 East Hanover Avenue, Morris Plains, New Jersey 07950. The address in England is 27 Andrew Close, Stoke Golding, Nuneaton CV13 6EL.

SINCLAIR USER Magazine. This excellent monthly magazine is a leading publication in England for owners of TS1000 computers. Subscriptions in the U.S. are handled by Gladstone Electronics (1585 Kenmore Avenue, Buffalo, New York 14217). Subscriptions are $40 per year in the U.S.; the magazine is less expensive in the U.K.

THE HARVARD GROUP. This organization (RD 2, Box 457, Bolton Road, Harvard, Massachusetts 01451) currently publishes two magazines on the TS1000. One, *Syntax*, has been in publication since 1980. It is $29 a year. It contains many useful articles, but far fewer than the two magazines listed above. There are fewer advertisers in *Syntax*, and reading the ads is one way to keep up with new products and programs. The new magazine from Harvard Group is *SQ* which is short for *Syntax Quarterly*. It is published four times a year and is nicely produced. Subscriptions are $15 for four issues. Although *SQ* is much higher in quality than *Syntax*, it will have to work hard to catch up with *Sync*. We did, however, feel that *SQ* was worth the $15 subscription price. It publishes programs, reviews of hardware, software, and books, articles on how to build accessories for your computer, and articles on using and managing the computer.

   SYNCHRO-SETTE. This is a magazine that also provides programs on cassette. A $40 subscription gets you 12 monthly issues of the magazine and 6 cassettes, each of which will contain at least six programs that run on the TS1000. It is available from S & S Company (388 W. Lake Street, Addison, Illinois 60101, 312-628-8955).

BOOKS AND BOOK PUBLISHERS

   A stroll through the computer section of your local bookstore is likely to show you just how popular the TS1000 really is. There are almost 100 different books about the TS1000 in current distribution. Few bookstores are likely to have more than three or four of them, but there is an increasing tendency for bookstores to carry a large number of computer books. In this section we will not try to review all the books currently on the market. There are too many, and the list would be out of date in a matter of months since new books are appearing regularly. Instead we will note some of the more active publishers of books about the TS1000. The publishers noted are likely to be bringing out new books as well. Many of the new books that appear each year are reviewed in magazines like *Sync* and *Sinclair User Magazine*. In addition, several of the suppliers listed in the next section add new books to their catalogs each year.

   Melbourne House Publishers (131 Trafalgar Road, Greenwich, London SE10 United Kingdom). Melbourne House bills itself as "the world's largest publishers of books and software for the Sinclair." It publishes books for virtually every level of user from beginner to expert.

dilithium Press (P.O. Box 606, Beaverton, Oregon 97075, 1-800-547-1842). dilithium is the publisher of this book and several more on the TS1000. The company has over 100 books, most of them at the beginning and intermediate level, on personal computing. You can get a free catalog by phoning them at the toll free number listed above.

Creative Computing Press (39 East Hanover Avenue, Morris Plains, New Jersey 07950, 1-800-631-8112). This company, now a division of the publishing giant Ziff-Davis, is the owner of *Sync* magazine as well as the very popular general magazine *Creative Computing*. It also publishes a number of books on the TS1000. Several of the books were originally published in England; others are adaptations of other Creative Computing books (e.g., *Computers for Kids* (Sinclair Edition) by Sally Larsen).

Reston Publishing Company (11480 Sunset Hills Road, Reston, Virginia 22090). This company is a division of Prentice-Hall. It has published American editions of several English books on the TS1000.

Young's Computer Publications (2 Woodland Way, Gosfield, Halstead, Essex CO9 1TH England). This group publishes the *ZX80/81 Register* which is a list and description of both hardware and software for the TS1000. At $9.50 this book is well worth the money. It is updated periodically and contains a listing of user groups in England and Europe. An American company, Micro Design Concepts (P.O. Box 280, Carrolton, Texas 75006) publishes a similar book called *Timex/Sinclair Sourcebook* for $5 plus $1.25 postage and handling. Another company, Atlanta Computer Products (P.O. Box 936, Norfolk, Virginia 23501) sells a Sourcebook on the TS1000 for $7 plus $1.25 for postage and handling.

SUPPLIERS

There are hundreds of companies that produce and/or sell products for the TS1000. A few, however, make or distribute a wide range of software, hardware, and publications. Some of the suppliers with a broad product line are listed in this section:

Memotech (7550 West Yale Avenue, Suite 220, Denver, Colorado 80227, 303-986-0016) manufactures and distributes several pieces of hardware.

Softsync (P.O. Box 480, Murray Hill Station, New York, New York 10156) markets many good programs and books for the TS1000.

Gladstone Electronics (901 Fuhrman Boulevard, Buffalo, New York 14203, 716-849-0735 and 1736 Avenue Road, Toronto, Ontario, 416-787-1448). Gladstone distributes hardware, software, and books. They have a nice fat catalog of supplies for the TS1000. This mail order company sells products made by many small (and large) companies. It is a convenient means of buying all sorts of products.

Sinclair Place (P.O. Box 2288, Redmond, Washington 98052). Like Gladstone this company distributes the products of many companies by mail. Sinclair Place carries quite a few products from British manufacturers that may be hard to get in the U.S.

Artic Computing (396 James Reckitt Avenue, Hull HU8 0JA United Kingdom). This company sells some hardware as well as software and books.

Mindware (70 Boston Post Road, Wayland, Massachusetts 01778). Mindware is another company that distributes software, hardware, and books for the TS1000.

ROM-PAC Applications (5921-A Alhambra, Norcross, Georgia 30093). This company markets a wide range of programs and some accessories for the TS1000.

JRS Software (19 Wayside Avenue, Worthing, Sussex BN13 3JU England, 0903-65691) is another distributor of hardware and software.

data-assette (56 South 3rd Street, Oxford, Pennsylvania 19363, 1-800-523-2909). This company markets a large assortment of software as well as hardware and publications. They expect you to pay $2.25 for their catalog but offer credit on your first order.

SOME FINAL WORDS

This is the final chapter in *How to Use Your Timex Sinclair Computer*. We hope you have found the book useful and that you continue to explore the possibilities of personal computing. If you have suggestions you feel would improve the next edition of the book please write us at dilithium Press. Happy computing!

Error Report Codes

The TS1000 computer tries to help you write usable BASIC programs in several ways. One way is through the use of report codes. If the computer encounters instructions in a BASIC program that it cannot understand or follow, it stops execution of the program and prints a report code in the bottom left corner of the screen. The standard format for the report code is #/# with the second number indicating the number of the program line where the problem occurred. The first number indicates the type of problem it encountered. Below is a list of the report codes used by the TS1000 and what they mean:

0. This report code tells you the program has been executed without an error.

1. **FOR NEXT**. You are using a **FOR NEXT** loop that is improperly set up.

2. UNDEFINED VARIABLE. You have told the computer to use a variable that the computer does not know about. Before a variable (e.g., A, B, B$, A$) is used you must use **LET** or **INPUT** to define it. Subscripted variables must be dimensioned before use. You will also get a 2 report code if your program gets to a line with a **NEXT** statement (e.g., 150 **NEXT** X) before the program encounters the line with **FOR** X = ...

3. INCORRECT SUBSCRIPT. You cannot use subscripts that are negative (e.g., A(−1) or subscripts that are larger than 65535).

4. OUT OF MEMORY. During execution, the program has been asked to do something that takes more memory than is

available. There may not even be enough memory for the complete report code (e.g., 4/4 could appear instead of 4/460). You must rewrite the program so that less memory is used or get more memory.

5. SCREEN FULL. If the program fills up the screen the computer will stop and a report code of 5 will be given. Use the key word **CONT** to tell the computer to continue executing the program or rewrite the program using the key word **SCROLL** to avoid the 5 report.

6. OVERFLOW. The computer has been asked to perform a calculation that produces an answer larger than it can handle. This computer cannot deal with numbers larger than about 1,000,000,000,000,000,000,000,000,000.

7. NO **GOSUB**. The computer has arrived at a **RETURN** instruction, but it did not arrive there because of a **GOSUB** instruction.

8. **INPUT**. You get an 8 report code if you try to use **INPUT** as a command. It can only be used as a statement (i.e., in a program).

9. **STOP**. The computer has encountered a **STOP** instruction in the program. It halts execution and gives a 9 report code.

A. FUNCTION PROBLEM. The A report code means the number used in a function is invalid.

B. INTEGER OUT OF RANGE. Many statements call for an integer or whole number (e.g., **RUN** 45, **GOSUB** 145, **PEEK** 14567). Most statements work with a particular range of numbers, but not with any number. The B code indicates the number to be used is out of the acceptable range for the statement.

If you get fancy and use an instruction such as **GOSUB** B/12 it is possible to get a number that is not an integer (e.g., 6.678). If that is the case the computer rounds the number off. A B report code indicates the rounding produced an integer that is not within the acceptable range for that key word.

C. **VAL** PROBLEM. You have tried to use the **VAL** function to convert a string to a numeric variable, but the string does not convert to a valid number.

D. BREAK USED. The D report code indicates program execution stopped because you pressed the **BREAK** key.

F. NO NAME. You have used the **SAVE** command and the name you gave the program is an empty string, that is, no name was given.

Index

ABS 93
accessory 107
AND 75
arrow keys 25
ARCCOS 94
ARCSIN 94
ARCTAN 94
ARITH 1.0 8
array 88
Artic Computing 120
ASCII 12

BASIC programming 4
battery backup 114
bit 12
BLACKJACK 6
Boolean expression 75
books 118
BREAK 58
business applications 8
byte 12
BYTE BACK MD-1 7

calculator mode 54
calculation order 69
CASH 8
cassette recorder connection 19, 38
CHECKBOOK BALANCER/
    CALCULATOR 7
CHR$ 95
CLEAR 55
clerical instructions 59
CLS 55
code 96
command 54
commas 59
COMPUTACALC 9
computer literacy 3
CONSTELLATION 7
CONT 57
control interfaces 113
control variable 79
copy 61
COS 94
CRAPS 6
Creative Computing 119

data-assette 120
dedicated addresses 100
DELETE key 26

dilithium Press 119
DIM 89
DIM and string variables 90
dimensional array 88
dimensional subscripted variable 90
dimensional variable 90

EDIT 56
editing 27
ENTER 54
ENTER key 25
error report codes 121
EXAM 8
execute 53
EXP 94
expansion boards 114

FAST 57
FOR NEXT 77
FRENCH VOCAB 8
functions 92

G cursor 33
Gladstone Electronics 120
GOTO 67
graphics 32
graphics aids 114
GROAN 7

HAMMURABI 6
Harvard Group 117
home applications 7

IF THEN 73
immediate mode 54
INKEY$ 67
INT 93
INT(eger) key 24
INPUT 64
insert 26
I/O ports 10

JRS Software 120

K 13
K cursor 25
keyboard 23
keyboards (add on) 109
keywords 52

L cursor 25
left arrow key 25
LET 63
LIFE 6
literal string 59
LIST 55
LLIST 56
LOAD 40
loading aids 115
logical operators 75
loop 79
LPRINT 61
LUNAR LANDER 6

machine language programming 5
magazine 117
math expression 69
matrix 88
Melbourne House Publishers 118
memory 12
memory (sources for extra) 108
memory map 99
memory map video 100
Memotech 119
Microace 1
Mindware 120
modem 113
MULTIPLICATION THREE-IN-A-ROW 8

nested loop 81
NEW 55
NEW key 37
NEXT 77
NOT 75
null string 68

one dimensional array 88
OR 75
organizers 116

PAUSE 55
PEEK 103
pi 93
pixels 85
PLOT 83
POKE 104
power connection 20
power supply 10
program control commands 54
program cursor 55
PRINT 59
PRINT AT 61
PRINT TAB 62
printers 111
publishers 118

quotation marks 59
quotation marks in strings 66

RAM 13
RAND 94
recorder connection 19, 38
REM 31

report code 71
Reston Publishing Company 119
right arrow key 25
RND 94
ROM 113
ROM-PACK applications 120
ROULETTE 6
RUN 54

S cursor 26
SAVE 47
screen dump 61
school applications 7
SCROLL 57
semicolon 59
SGN 93
SIN 94
Sinclair Place 120
Sinclair User's Magazine 117
SKI RUN 7
SLOT MACHINE 6
SLOW 57
SOFTSYNC 120
SQR 93
statement 53
step 77
STOP 58
string 59
string comparison 74
string functions 94
string variable 63
subroutine 81
subscripted variables 88
SUPERINVASION 6
suppliers 119
SYNC Magazine 117
SYNCHRO-SETTE 118

TAB 62
TAN 94
tape recorder connection 19, 38
television connection 17, 38
THEN 73
Timex Sinclair 1000 1
tone control 40
trigonometric functions 94
TS 1000 1
types of numbers 70

UNPLOT 83
USR 105

VAL 96
variables 63
volume control 40
VU-CALC 9

Young Computer Publications 119

ZETATREK 6
ZXCHESS 6
ZX80 1
ZX81 1